DOES *GOD* HAVE E-MAIL?

DOES *GOD* HAVE E-MAIL?

Barbara Davey

A collection of short stories and essays
to warm the heart, touch the soul and nourish the spirit
with loving narratives of everyday miracles . . .

Rutledge Books, Inc.   Danbury, CT

Interior design by Sharon Gelfand

Rutledge Books, Inc.
107 Mill Plain Road
Danbury, CT 06811
www.rutledgebooks.com

Manufactured in the United States of America

Davey, Barbara
    Does God Have E-Mail?

    ISBN: 1-58244-137-5

    1. Inspirational Essays. 2. Collection.

Library of Congress Catalog Number: 2001088290

Also by Barbara Davey

The Ballad of a Norwegian Prince

Prunilla's Revenge

Contents

Introduction

Does God have E-Mail? Probably not, but then, He doesn't need it, for He communicates with every one of us everyday without it. The challenge, and often the difficulty, lies in recognizing His "instant messages" which often appear as seemingly ordinary occurrences during the course of our daily lives.

Does God Have E-Mail is a collection of some of these messages which I refer to as *IMs* or "instant miracles" I have witnessed in my own life.

After reading these narrations, I hope you, too, will recognize some of the same messages in your own life, for you, too, have been receiving them every day.

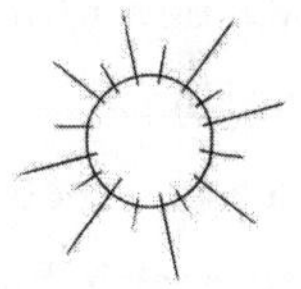

Our Gardening Angel

Have you noticed there seems to be a proliferation of celestial beings celebrated here on earth lately? Browse through any bookstore or greeting card display and you will have to agree that angels certainly seem to be among us.

Personally, the concept of "an angel watching over me" has been a familiar theme. I grew up believing there was a guardian angel for everyone. Recently, however, I am convinced that, like their earthly counterparts, angels come in many sizes, shapes, and forms, and practice many professions. And one of them is gardening.

This year, there is a new angel tending the gardens in Paradise. His name is Hans Becker, my father-in-law, who recently joined the heavenly grounds-keeping crew. And, since his arrival, I cannot help but ponder, have flowers always been so lush, so colorful and so vibrant, or has Hans been working his miracles from above?

I will never forget the day my husband and I received the news that Hans had been diagnosed with one of life's most dreaded diseases—metastatic colon cancer. We were devastated. Though Hans was in his seventies, we had never thought of him in terms of age. Rather, he seemed of a different dimension, an almost gnome-like creature, who delighted in nature, flowers, and the outdoors. A being who was unencumbered by earthly restrictions, such as age, sickness, and physical limitations.

A gentle soul, Hans communicated best using no words at all. Rather, his hands served as a unique conduit—instruments that healed, sowed, and nurtured. Flowers, plants, and animals responded to his touch in an inexplicable manner. Instinctually, they seemed to know these were gentle hands. Instruments that could be trusted to mend broken wings, to nourish barren soil, and to replenish much needed water.

I always found it rather endearing that Hans would scoff at those who wasted their money by purchasing expensive "bottled" water, opting to quench his own thirst directly from the tap. However, he spent countless hours collecting rainwater. His flowers, plants, gardens, and birds would be refreshed with God's water, never to be subjected to chemicals and metallic-tasting substances.

"They know the difference," he would tell me. And witnessing the results—lush gardens, fragrant flowers, and birdbaths overflowing with feathered friends—one would have to agree.

Neighborhood children responded to Hans in a similar manner.

Like birds, they seemed to flock to his side for no apparent reason. He never bribed them with sweets, toys or stories. In fact, I
doubt they spoke to each other much at all. Rather, children of
all ages would silently follow him. Watching him feed the birds,
water the flowers, till the soil, they shadowed his movements.
They seemed especially fascinated with an antique baby carriage he had converted into a planter. Filled with tropical flowers, Hans and the children wheeled the planter around the garden several times each day, strategically placing it in key loca-
tions to maximize the amount of sunlight these fragile plants
required to thrive.

Looking back, I think it was his simple creed, embracing a life so
unencumbered by material possessions and so tied to the natural cycle of life, that made his final illness so difficult for us to
endure. When confronted with this diagnosis, high-tech, state-
of-the-art therapies claimed center stage. There was little time to
collect rainwater, mend broken wings, and wheel planters while
undergoing months of radiation treatments.

During those last few weeks, I remember thinking how out-of-
place Hans looked in the regional oncology center. Draped in a
hospital gown, he appeared to shrink visibly. For years, I had
naively believed that Hans had been the caregiver, the nurturer,
the healer of nature. But now, I realized it was a reciprocal relationship. His soul craved that gardening garb, his spirit needed
that environment, as much as his body required oxygen. Cut off
from these spiritual lifelines, he was lost.

Watching him surrounded by steel and chrome, while encased

within the sterile atmosphere of the hospital, my heart ached. He reminded me of E. T., a benevolent displaced being, wanting to go home, but not knowing how to get there.

Finally, the doctors with all their state-of-the-art technology pronounced there was nothing more they could do. Hans could leave the hospital. Though we could not restore him to his gardens, we could take him home, and we did not waste a minute in doing so.

In the remaining months, as difficult as they seemed, a more natural sequence of events unfolded. Hospice nurses eased all of us into a more humane pattern of life. Each day was viewed as an opportunity to see a sunrise, smell a flower, or hold each others' hands.

During those precious days, I found myself collecting rainwater to refresh the flowers near Hans's bedside. If I had any remaining water, I would return to his gardens and tend to the flowers. I never did, however, master the technique of wheeling the baby-carriage-turned-planter around the gardens. That remained in a corner in the yard, catching what sunlight it could.

Hans died on a beautiful June day. The sky was blue and crystal clear. My husband and I had just been at his bedside. He didn't speak to us. He opened his eyes and waved good-by. Those marvelous, gentle, miraculous hands. I like to think of those hands saying, "I'll be going now. There's a beautiful garden that needs me. Auf-wiedersehen or until we meet again."

Afterward, as the hospice nurse tended to his body, I fled to his gardens, the home of his soul. My tears were flowing so heavily, I didn't notice at first. Then I saw it . . .

Settled in the middle of the garden, bathed in golden rays of sunshine, sat the planter, and every flower was turning its head to the heavens.

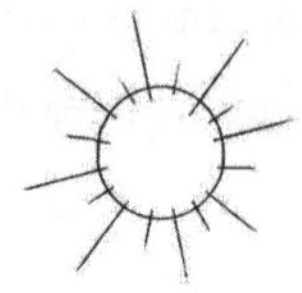

WINIFRED'S LEGACY OF LOVE

People like Winifred Austin Fisher made me nervous. As the director of fundraising at a large urban hospital, I would be eternally grateful to the woman whose last will and testament lay scattered across my desk, but at the same time, her lifestyle frightened me. Perhaps because it reflected my own too closely.

Born in Hyde Park, Massachusetts in 1910, Winifred was the only child of Austin and Mary Fisher. A steamfitter, her father died in 1925 of scarlet fever, leaving little in the way of assets. Two years later, Winifred broke with the tradition of the day by gaining employment as a bookkeeper. At seventeen, she was not only a "working woman," but had the added distinction of being the sole support of her mother.

For the next fifty years, Winifred spent a good part of her life crunching numbers. She never married, had no children, and after her mother died in 1952, lived alone. At the time of her own death,

Winifred had no living relatives and she bequeathed nearly $1 million to local charities. The largest portion was left to our hospital.

"Ah, Winnie," I sighed, looking through her file, "why didn't you spend some of that money on yourself?" From what I could ascertain, her last address was a three-room apartment in a four-story walkup. And the building itself was located in one of the least desirable sections of the city.

Several days later I met with her attorney, a distinguished elderly gentleman, to discuss a fitting memorial for our benefactor. "She was a very private person, mild-mannered but decisive," he recalled. "She knew exactly what she wanted. She was conscientious, diligent, thrifty, and rarely indulged herself. She had a deep feeling for charitable causes, particularly in the health care field. Use her money wisely."

But who was Winifred Austin Fisher? I wanted to scream at the lawyer. What were her dreams? Her fears? Was she ever in love? Did she wear purple? Or incredible hats? Had she ever seen the Eiffel Tower? Or Tibet? Did she sing in the shower? Or walk barefoot in the park? Who was she? I wanted to know.

Unfortunately, I'll probably never find out. While the timing of her death prevented me from obtaining any personal information, the timing of her bequest could not have been better. The hospital had recently undertaken a major building campaign, and, thanks to Winifred, the project would now be completed on time and within budget. After speaking with her attorney, we decided to apply a large portion of her contribution to the pediatric emergency area.

As a former public relations professional, I pulled out all stops to make Winifred's donation a media blitz. At the dedication ceremony, reporters were out in force, and one major news station in Manhattan sent a film crew. The following day, every newspaper printed her picture beneath a banner headline reading, "Heaven Sent."

While I was pleased that Winifred had finally received the recognition she so much deserved, nothing could compare to the way I felt when I discovered the first patient treated in the new pediatrics area was a little boy named Austin. A benevolent force was at work somewhere, and I sensed that Winifred was pleased we had used her money wisely.

But Winifred's legacy to me was so much more than medical equipment, bricks, mortar, and a lucrative bottom line. I thought about her constantly that first year, and began to make subtle changes in my own life "in the name of Winnie."

That year, I bought a new wardrobe in vibrant colors, relinquishing my traditional beige and navy. I booked a trip to Paris (solo like Lucky Lindy!), forsaking the Jersey shore. I began to investigate several charities, and initiated a program for women with cancer. Later that fall, contemplating a career move, I attended a seminar on eldercare. The presenter was a rakish-looking man, whose command of language captivated the audience. During the break, we began a conversation over the coffee pot.

"You work at the hospital, don't you?" he asked. Without waiting for my reply, he continued, "I recognize you from that dedication ceremony last year. You did a great job. Winnie would have loved it. I knew her, you know. I used to visit her quite often. How did you know she loved children?"

Looking into the eyes of the man who was to become my husband, I answered, "I just did. But can you tell me, did she like purple hats?"

This story was originally published in *Chocolate for a Woman's Blessings*, Simon & Schuster, 2000.

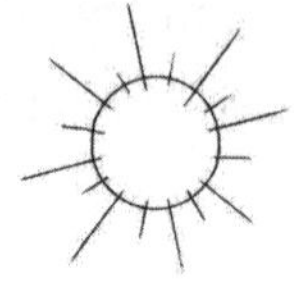

HOME IS WHERE THE HEARTH IS

There's an old Gaelic expression that states, "May the roof above you and the hearth before you always be your own . . ." And reflecting upon the history of war-torn, famished Ireland, it is not difficult to understand why a safe haven, a home, was so highly regarded by the Irish.

Such were my thoughts as I surveyed the brownstone on West Eighteenth Street, bordering New York City's Greenwich Village. The day was cold, gray, and dreary, as I stood outside the wrought iron gate surrounding the home. At the turn of the century, this modest building meant the world to Maggie O'Connor, an immigrant from County Clare. One of my biggest regrets was that I never had the opportunity to meet dear Maggie, who had been my great-grandmother.

Bursting with optimism, eighteen-year-old Maggie landed at Ellis Island in 1892 with little more than five dollars in her pocket and the clothes on her back. But she wasted no time lamenting how little she had, and promptly secured a position that afternoon as a cook's helper in a wealthy Park Avenue household.

A year later, she married a fellow Irisher, a handsome long-shoreman from Donegal. The two set up housekeeping on the third floor of the brownstone which now stood before me. Seven years and five babies later, he was killed, tragically, crushed between the dock and some itinerant cargo.

How often have I wondered what thoughts must have gone through her mind at this time . . . Did she consider returning to Ireland? Putting her children up for adoption? Turning to her mainstay, the Catholic Church? I like to imagine her squaring her narrow shoulders, jutting her chin forward, and swallowing her fears. Women in my family have always been pillars of strength, and I like to attribute that trait to Maggie.

My grandmother remembered little about her father. What was very clear to her, however, was that shortly after his death, the family moved "downstairs." In hindsight, it seems that without her husband's income, Maggie could no longer afford the upstairs apartment, and she lost no time in relocating her young family to the basement quarters. Once situated, she convinced the owner of the brownstone to accept a bartered arrangement. Every morning, she promised to fill each open heating grate of the twelve units above with coal, then prepare breakfast and later dinner for all of the boarders. In exchange, she and her children could live in the basement quarters rent-free.

The owner must have agreed as my grandmother recalls Maggie herded the five children into that "downstairs" apartment. But my grandmother's memories were not depressing. Rather than "dark and damp," my grandmother described their home to be "light and bright." And she said that every day brought a new adventure.

But if Maggie had painted a rosy picture for her children, in reality her life was one of continuous work and little leisure. Every morning, she carried buckets of coal to the twelve families living upstairs. Then, while keeping an eye on her own brood, she would prepare breakfast for the boarders, serving them in the large dining area. Her own children would then eat in the kitchen, and my grandmother recalled that leftovers had never tasted so delicious.

Several hours each afternoon, Maggie worked as a laundress, and the children accompanied her to various homes along Seventh Avenue. During the late afternoon, they returned to the boarding house to prepare dinner. As time was a commodity not to be squandered, she filled the evening hours taking in "piece-work," sewing by the fire.

If times seemed hard, she never complained. There was food on the table and a roof over her head. In Ireland she had neither, for famine and poverty were everywhere.

So many times in my life I have thought about Maggie, my great-grandmother, and how hard she worked. For it was through her back-backing labor that my grandmother was able to learn a trade, my mother was able to attend college, and I was able to obtain a graduate degree. Because of her sacrifices, I had inherited a life of more ease and luxury.

Over the years, when I enjoyed a relaxing weekend, I often wished I could spend part of it with Maggie. Perhaps we could have enjoyed tea and scones at a five-star hotel, had a manicure and massage at an exclusive spa, or taken in a movie or a play at an upscale theatre. But, somehow, I know she would not have enjoyed these experiences . I imagine she would have been nervous, frightened, and even suspicious of such pampering and leisurely activity. I can almost hear her politely declining my invitations, and escaping to the safety of her basement apartment, her familiar mending nestled in her lap.

So deep were my thoughts as I stared at the brownstone I had not noticed the drizzle had quickly become a downpour. As I struggled with my umbrella, the present owner opened the door. He seemed to be of a gentle nature, smiled shyly, and asked if he could assist me.

"Oh, I'm sorry," I stammered. "I was just admiring your home. Someone I knew used to live here a very long time ago."

He brightened visibly and asked if I would like to take a look inside. He seemed to be quite proud of the brownstone. "I'd love to," I responded, climbing the porch steps.

As I walked through the large foyer, dining room, and parlor, I could appreciate his pride. The home was magnificent and had been restored to its Victorian splendor. But my interest was not on the main floor. "Would I be able to see the basement?" I asked.

The owner smiled. "The basement? Now, that's an unusual request. How did you know that is my favorite part of the house?"

The stairs were located behind the kitchen, and as I descended, I thought of dear Maggie hauling endless buckets of coal up these very same steps.

Reaching the bottom, I gasped. Despite the gray afternoon and the rain beating against the high basement windows, the entire area seemed to be bathed in light. With overstuffed chairs and ottomans surrounding an open hearth, the room felt like a homey refuge. But there was more. An inexplicable, benevolent force seemed to permeate the room—as if it were almost a holy place, a place which only knew love.

On the mantle was a Greek statue, and I inquired about it. "It's Hestia, the goddess of the home and hearth," the owner answered. "She watches over this house. While I love what she represents, I am not fond of the name Hestia. It seems a bit too formal, a bit cold, doesn't it?"

"Have you ever considered calling her Maggie?" I asked him. And suddenly, rays of sunlight streamed through the basement windows.

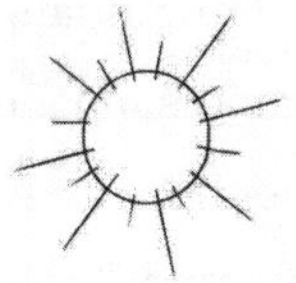

An Angel on a Park Bench

Our telephone conversation lasted exactly four minutes and seventeen seconds—I know because I asked the telephone company for a log of the call. However, had I known that would be the last time I would ever speak to my beloved grandfather, I would have never hung up the phone.

While the natural cycle of life should have prepared me for his eventual death, the thought of losing him was something I would never allow myself to consider. Throughout his life, Grandpa seemed to defy the conventions of the aging process. Hale, hearty, robust, and quick-witted were attributes he personified—well into his nineties. He was my confidante, my mentor, and my best friend until a cerebral hemorrhage claimed him instantaneously, leaving me with a hole through my heart, soul, and spirit.

In Grandpa's eyes, I always felt extraordinarily special. I was his

first granddaughter, but he was not one to spoil me. With an elo-
quent manner of speaking and a magnificent carriage, he attracted
attention in every arena. Whether we were in a restaurant, a
supermarket line or a doctor's office, people gravitated toward
him and I loved being at his side. Grandpa could walk with
princes, but he never lost the common touch. He lived by the
serenity prayer, accepting what could not be changed, while
bravely trying to improve what he could. However, even as a
young child, I always sensed that he heeded a Higher Power.
His example was his greatest gift to me.

In the weeks that followed his death, I lived a numbing existence. In retrospect, I felt the only purpose those first few
months served were to hollow out my heart further, only to
make more room for the pain that followed. I felt as if I stag-
gered through the days, only to be tortured with thoughts of
him throughout the night.

I don't recall when I started walking to a nearby park. I do
remember, however, I needed to physically escape the mental
anguish I was experiencing. I could not even begin to comprehend that he was gone. He would no longer enter a room,
answer the telephone, share a meal. During those months, my
only objective was to exhaust myself physically by day, to
ensure my nights would be given over to a numbing sleep.

Soon, my walking pattern became routine. A few miles to our
neighborhood park, with a brief rest on the same bench overlook-
ing a duck pond. An elderly man often sat on the same bench on
the opposite side. Neither of us ever spoke to the other, but I some-

how sensed we were both seeking a similar peace in the silence.

Months passed, and, though I cannot be certain when, these excursions began to quiet my heart. I felt that some kind of change was happening. The old man smoked a pipe, and the tobacco reminded me of a time long ago when my grandfather used to smoke one, too. I had forgotten. Perhaps the aroma triggered something, but I was transported back to a happier time. I remembered myself as a child reading the Sunday comics with Grandpa, playing with wooden blocks, and telling stories while eating canned fruit .

Throughout the next few months, other images flooded my memory. School graduations, holiday celebrations, birthdays, and summer vacations from long ago were relived while sitting on that park bench. Again, neither I nor that old man had ever spoken, but somehow I knew my gradual healing was related to the time spent on that bench.

One morning I remember waking up and the oppressive weight that seemed to be lying on my heart had lightened. It was then I recalled a dream I had had hours earlier. My beloved grandfather was there. I recognized him immediately, but he was different—almost better, but in another time and sphere. He looked a little peculiar, though. As if he were a bit disturbed with me, a bit confused. At the time, I couldn't quite place the look on his face, but I knew I had seen it before.

It came to me later that day as I sat on the park bench. There, gently surrounded by the aroma of tobacco as my elderly companion puffed on his pipe, I remembered. Thirty-five ago, my grandparents had taken a trip to Ireland. I hadn't wanted my grandfather to leave me and I carried on horribly, crying out how much I would miss him. He had been disappointed in my behavior then, and that same look had been on his face.

"Why are you acting like this?" he had asked me. "I'm only going away for a short time. I'll see you again very soon. Stop that."

Looking back over my behavior the past year, I could almost hear that same admonishment. But there seemed to be a new twist to his message this time. Now, he seemed to be saying, "Let me go. I am finally home and I am happy. But I am disturbed with you. It's not your time yet. When you're ready to come home, I'll be here. I am already waiting for you . . ." That realization hit me like a thunderbolt. I sat on the park bench for quite some time. Finally, with the sun setting, I buttoned my coat and started home. It was only then I realized the old man had left.

From that day, while I continued to miss my grandfather deeply, my heart didn't seem quite so heavy. I could even smile when I remembered his perfect diction, erect posture, and witty sayings. I continued my walks to the park, but I never saw the old man again. One day, I asked the park rangers if they had seen him.

The three men looked at each other, and then at me. Finally, one of them said, "We're not quite sure what you mean, miss. The three of us have watched you sit on that same park bench every day for nearly a year. But you have always been alone. We have never once seen that old man you're asking about . . ."

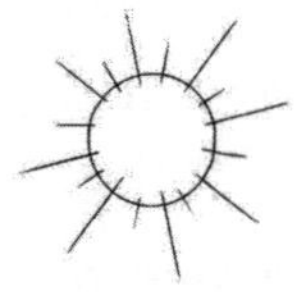

In Sickness and in Health...

Have you ever noticed that what seemed to be an inconsequential, insignificant detail at the time, sometimes becomes a turning point in your life? That's what happened to me the day I met Heinz and Elisabeth, and from that time hence, my life has never been quite the same.

To back up a bit, my dear grandmother spent the last years of her life in a skilled nursing facility. While not exactly the way many of us envision our final days, Grandmother was comfortable, though confused, seemed content, and was cared for by a staff who personified compassion. Nevertheless, I made a commitment to visit her several times each week. Though she no longer recognized me, I felt it essential to remember her.

On one particular visit, Grandmother and I altered our usual routine. On a whim, I decided to wheel her to the western end of the building, though her room was situated on the opposite side of the complex. It was on that very day we met Heinz and Elisabeth.

The western end of the building opened to a lovely courtyard, a mirror image of the eastern side Grandmother and I usually frequented. Sitting in a wheelchair, covered with a soft afghan, was a lovely, ethereal-looking woman. Her attention seemed focused on the elderly gentleman standing before her. Impeccably dressed, he was playing a hauntingly beautiful melody on a violin.

Immediately I stopped pushing the wheelchair and listened. Even my grandmother seemed moved by the music. The melody continued for several minutes before the man stopped and bowed politely to his audience of three. Enthusiastically, I applauded and shook his hand. That was my first encounter with Heinz, a musical virtuoso, and Elisabeth, his wife of sixty-five years who was suffering from Alzheimer's disease.

Throughout the next six months, Heinz and Elisabeth became an integral part of the life my grandmother and I shared at the nursing facility. Through the course of our conversations, I learned that Heinz had studied music in Vienna. At the time, Elisabeth was an aspiring opera singer. They met at a concert, fell in love, and married. Before either could achieve their dream of performing in Vienna, they were forced to flee Europe in the wake of the Second World War. Arriving in America, both had found menial jobs in various factories, but neither had forgotten their first love—music.

Tragedy had struck the couple several years earlier, as Elisabeth began retreating into a world of her own. "She never speaks anymore, she never sings," sighed Heinz. "She had the voice of an angel, but it's been silenced. I don't even think she hears my music."

I wanted to comfort him, but I respected him too much to lie. In the months I had known them, Elisabeth had never spoken, and although she looked at him, she seemed to have an attitude of polite indifference. Both she and my grandmother seemed to be trapped between two worlds. Their bodies were somehow still tethered to this one, while their spirits had left long ago.

Nevertheless, Heinz continued to perform for us. As he played, I watched his marvelous hands. Gnarled with arthritis, freckled with age, they were magical as he coaxed the sweetest sounds from his violin. On his left pinkie, he wore a thin gold ring.

"It was my father's," he explained, "the only thing I have from the old country. I remember the day my father gave it to me. 'Take it, keep it,' he said, 'until we meet again.' That was the last time I saw him. I've worn it every day since. First on my ring finger, now on my little one."

One weekend Heinz came to the nursing home and seemed quite excited. "Guess what, my liechen," he exclaimed. "I've been asked to play in a concert next weekend. Though it's only a local symphony, it's quite an honor. I'll have a small solo, and the concert will be broadcast over public television."

I shared his enthusiasm. What an achievement at eighty-five

years of age! I found some plastic glasses and a pitcher of lemonade at the nurses' station and proposed a toast. "Here's to Heinz and the fulfillment of his dreams—a little delayed perhaps, but realized all the same!"

The evening of the concert, I offered to look in on Elisabeth for him. After my grandmother was settled for the night, I walked to the western end of the building to Elisabeth's room. The moment I saw her, I knew something was different. She was sitting up in her bed, looking almost agitated. Knowing her as calm and compliant, the change was startling. I tried in vain to soothe her to sleep, but she would have none of it. Her eyes seemed to snap at me. Finally, she swallowed hard, and in a raspy voice I heard her say, "I can't sleep. I'm going home tonight. Home with my Heinz."

Stunned, as I had never heard her voice, I sat with her for nearly an hour. But she would not lie down, and refused to speak again. Her eyes remained open and alert. She kept looking at the door as if she were expecting Heinz to enter at any moment. Finally, exhausted, I went home. I was anxious to tell Heinz I had finally heard his Elisabeth's voice.

However, I never had the opportunity. Heinz died that same night, minutes after the concert. Those who were with him said he simply put down his violin, and collapsed with a beautiful smile still on his face. I heard the account the following morning when I arrived at the nursing home. That same night, Elisabeth had slipped away, too. The night nurse had heard a cry from her room. When she entered, she saw Elisabeth sitting up in bed, reaching for something. By the time the nurse had gotten to her side, Elisabeth was gone.

"It's not that uncommon, " one of the nurses told me. "When two people are together as long as those two were, they have a special kind of connection. When one goes, the other can sometimes sense it. We see that a lot here."

With that, I merely nodded and took my last walk to the western building. I knew I would never make this trip again, but I had wanted to see Elisabeth's room one final time. As I peeked in, I saw her bed had been stripped and the staff had already tidied the room. Her clothing and personal belongings were still there. I walked over to the chair beside her bed where I had sat with her only hours before. Something on her night table caught my eye. I walked closer and looked. There, gleaming in the sunlight, was a gold ring—the same one Heinz had always worn.

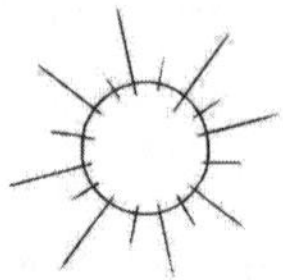

Launching a Dream
on Lobsters

Defining moments are not supposed to occur in the local fish market. Rather, they should be created on a wedding day, during the birth of a child, or at a long-awaited graduation. In addition, these life-altering experiences are supposed to be planned for, anticipated, or at least somewhat expected.

However, as I walked to our neighborhood fishery with my husband of twenty years, a sense of foreboding overshadowed me. I kept thinking, something is up and I don't think I want to hear it. With seagulls squawking overhead and water lapping against the shore, he told me he wanted to leave his job. Break out on his own. Live by his own lights. While he was concerned with leaving the security of a pension, health benefits, a terrific staff, an expense account, and other "perks," this was something he just had to do.

My stomach churned. At forty-something, I had assumed we had finally gotten to the point where, financially at least, things had eased up. For two decades, I had paid my dues by clipping coupons, shopping sales, and taking public transportation. Over the years, I had also prepaid our mortgage, kept a tight rein on our credit cards, and funded our IRAs. Finally, I could treat myself to a manicure without guilt, hire a cleaning service for the heavy household chores, and employ a local teen to maintain the lawn and shovel the snow.

Initially, however, it had been difficult for me to adjust to these "pleasures." Although I work ten-hour days, Monday through Friday, I continued to work that infamous "second shift" at home until my forty-second birthday. Standing in that fish market, I could see the pleasurable parts of my life begin to evaporate, just like the steam escaping from the enormous pots of chowder.

Then, my eyes traveled to the lobster tanks against the wall. Like the unfortunate inhabitants, I realized that as the primary breadwinner, I, too, would be imprisoned within my current career. In addition, I would be responsible for carrying the family's health benefits, and I resented my husband for putting me in this position.

The look on my face must have given him an idea of what was going on in my head because he suddenly looked like a remorseful five-year-old kid. "Oh, no, I'm sorry. Forget I even mentioned it," he pleaded. "It was just a stupid dream I had. Just forget it." And he tried to force a smile.

But somehow I knew it wasn't just a stupid dream. It was real. And it was something he had been working up the courage to tell me for quite some time. I looked at him carefully. Somehow

I knew the way I handled the next few minutes would impact the rest of our lives. I tried a weak smile.

"I've crunched some numbers, " he said tentatively, "and while I know that initially, the financial burden will fall to you, I really believe that in one year, I'll recoup my current salary. Then, I'd like you to cut back. Maybe part-time?"

Part-time? I thought. That did sound nice. Before I could respond, the clerk behind the counter was asking me for my order. "The usual right, Mrs. B? Two pounds of flounder and a quart of chowder?"

"No, give us two of your best lobsters, and throw in a dozen shrimp," I smiled. "I have a feeling we're coming into a windfall."

And somehow I knew we would.

This story was originally published in *Chocolate for a Woman's Soul Sequel*, Simon & Schuster, 2001.

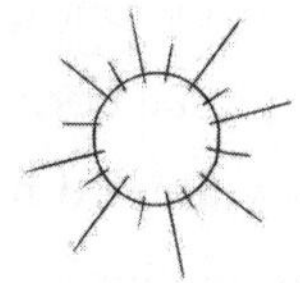

In Search of Mermaids . . .

On clear, crisp evenings when the stars appear so close you could reach up and touch them, I cannot help but think of Annabelle Wilson. Waiflike, almost ethereal, Annabelle seemed to float into our high school creative writing class in 1970. Swathed in voluminous dresses, her long hair pinned in a chignon, she seemed almost magical to us ninth-graders. We knew she was a graduate student although she seemed younger than we were—too innocent, too wide-eyed, and too trusting.

"Write what you feel, write what's in your heart," she used to say to us. "Never be afraid to reach for the stars. Touch them for those who cannot."

Born in her mother's midlife, Annabelle was named for her two grandmothers, both of whom had left this world long before her birth. Even her own father died before she reached her second birthday. My own mother used to say that change of life babies

were extraordinary. As they had been with God for so long waiting to be born, they brought a piece of heaven with them when
they arrived here on earth. I had never paid much attention to
my mother's tales, but with regard to Annabelle, I sensed she
may have been onto something. In my mind's eye, I can still see
Annabelle standing near an opened window catching rays of
sunlight. She looked almost translucent—somewhere between
this world and the next.

Annabelle stayed with us throughout the year, painting pictures
with her words. She had an uncanny way of unleashing the creative talents in the most unlikely candidates: Karl Jurgenson,
who still works in the service station owned by his grandfather,
writes poetry in his spare time . . . Lisa Anne Puleo, who married and produced five children within six years of our high
school graduation, claims writing short stories has preserved
her sanity . . . and Richard Bodekowski, who enlisted in the US
Marine Corps at eighteen, still keeps a daily journal, where he
"writes what he feels, and touches the stars every day." Each one
of them credits his or her creativity to Annabelle's influence.

When Annabelle left us in June, there was no doubt in our minds
she would go on to write the proverbial great American novel, a
five-act play worthy of a Tony, or a slim volume of exquisite
poetry. At the very least, she would continue to inspire others by
teaching creative writing—twirling about the room in delight as
a student recited an opening paragraph.

But Annabelle would not write that book, pen that play, create
that poetry, or even teach that writing class for a long time. That

summer, her mother developed Alzheimer's disease, and required constant care. Annabelle needed money quickly.

Putting her creative dreams on hold, she landed a job in a high-powered advertising firm. I could not imagine her within those corporate corridors housed in the glass skyscraper downtown. I could not visualize her developing slick brochures, editing corporate jargon, and promoting superficial merchandise. Every time I saw that office tower, I thought of it as a steel cage, which imprisoned a beautiful wild bird.

Ironically, I had landed a new job in that same building some ten years later. During my first week, I had wanted to visit Annabelle—I hadn't seen her since the ninth grade. But with all the confusion of starting a new job, I postponed the visit. That weekend, while reading the morning newspaper, I noticed an obituary. Annabelle's mother had died. On Monday morning I walked into Annabelle's office before my own. I needed to offer my condolences. I needed to see her.

When the elevator left me off on the sixteenth floor, I walked through the glass doors and located her cubicle. Several of her coworkers where milling about the area, shaking their heads. "We can't believe it. She just left. Why would she resign now? She knew she was going to be promoted this week . . ."

As I looked at the pitiful gray cubicle that had housed Annabelle for the past decade, I cringed. A cold drab prism, with barely enough room for a metal desk and straight-backed chair. There were no windows, no sunlight, and these so-called coworkers who had spent ten years with Annabelle were genuinely confused. While they continued to ruminate on how could she leave, I kept asking how did she ever stay? Even more disturbing to me now was what had happened to her during this ordeal? Had ten years in this quasi-prison broken her spirit? When I thought of her pirouetting in delight throughout our ninth grade classroom, my eyes filled with tears.

While attempting to blink them away, I stared up at the ceiling. At first, it was difficult to discern, but they were there. Five tiny gold stars pasted upon the ceiling above the cubicle. Seeing them, I smiled, and somehow knew at that very moment that Annabelle was okay.

"Where has Annabelle gone?" asked a voice I initially did not recognize as my own. "She's gone to search for mermaids, ride winged horses, and touch the stars." I am certain her former coworkers thought I was crazy, but I knew no one in that ninth grade class back in 1970 would ever doubt me.

This story was originally published in *Chocolate for a Teen's Soul: Life-Changing Stories for Young Women About Growing Wise and Growing Strong*, Simon & Schuster, 2000.

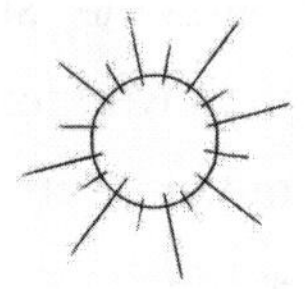

THE DAILY GRIND

Pinpointing the exact moment I began feeling a bit sorry for Shelley, a waitress in our neighborhood diner, would be difficult. For she had been a fixture in my life for as long as I can remember. Even more perplexing is identifying the time my perception of Shelley started to shift, and I even considered that perhaps she was one of the more fortunate ones. However, even the most casual observer would have to agree that carrying heavy trays of scrambled eggs, pouring endless cups of coffee, and wiping down countless countertops of breakfast residue is not the easiest way to pay the rent—especially when you're a grandmother pushing fifty.

Yet, every morning Shelley arrived at the diner before 5 a.m., greeting the regulars and newcomers alike with her customary smile and a cup of steaming joe. A quicker study I have never seen, as low-fat milk, sugar substitute, or decaffeinated blends, as preferred by each respective customer, would appear before them as they settled themselves into their favorite chair or stool. I often wondered if any of the customers ever realized how this familiar routine may have favorably altered their mornings, resulting in a more productive, satisfying day.

Throughout the years, I often felt like a voyeur as I watched Shelley serving breakfast to harried schoolteachers, professionals, so-called "captains of industry," and homemakers who occasionally treated themselves to a hot breakfast, prepared and served by someone else.

During these times, I wondered if Shelley somehow felt as if the world were passing her by—especially as she continued to pour coffee for patrons who seemed younger and more affluent each year. After all, they were taking the real world on, setting it on fire, while Shelley's career aspirations seemed to take her no further than the diner's kitchen.

But then I recalled an incident one morning when my thoughts began to shift. Sitting in my usual corner, I noticed a young woman dressed in a designer suit, clutching an expensive leather briefcase. I recognized her as a reporter on one of the local cable stations and a newcomer to the diner. She seemed quite agitated, as she waited for her coffee to go. Drumming her fingers on the counter, she let out an exasperated sigh as she watched Shelley patiently taking an elderly customer's order.

"Jeezes, I don't have all day to sit around a diner," she muttered, checking her watch. Observing the drama, I noticed the woman flip open her day planner. Watching her, I mused that she probably had double-booked meetings, set impossible deadlines, and scheduled too many meetings. "I'll have to clone myself to get through today," I heard her mutter.

Then I noticed Shelley, who had managed to prepare the woman's coffee, placing it neatly in a brown bag, receipt stapled to the rolled down top. Oblivious to Shelley's actions, the woman continued to check her planner. All the time, Shelley nodded in sympathy to the elderly patron as he recited his physical malady of the day. While listening to him, Shelley continued to refill coffee cups, replenish a sugar container, and clear the counter.

Exasperated, the young woman finally slammed her day planner closed. I held my breath, prepared to listen to her berate Shelley. Thankfully, she never got that far, as Shelley slid the brown bag toward her, and offered that familiar smile of hers. Grabbing the bag, the woman threw some change at the register and stormed out of the diner. Weeks later, I read the woman was leaving the network to "pursue other interests," though the word on the street was otherwise.

About a month later, I remember overhearing a conversation between Shelley and one of her "regulars," a pleasant, middle-aged woman who was determined to shift her relationship with her boss from a professional one to one of a personal nature. Initially, the woman had entered the diner with a distinguished gentleman. They had shared a friendly conversation over cups of coffee. Picking up the check with a polite nod, the man left. Upon his departure, the woman turned to Shelley.

"I've been with him for eighteen years," she sighed, as Shelley refilled her cup. "I've helped him build his business from a fledging three-person operation to the largest architectural firm in this area. No one has worked harder than I have."

Then, realizing she may have insulted Shelley, she added, "Oh please forgive me, I know you work hard, too, but it's just that I have been so involved with every aspect of the business. During a big project I'm there weekends, holidays, summers. I have taken such good care of him and everything associated with the business . . . Lately, I have been getting this funny feeling that he is considering marriage again, and, well, I feel it is finally my turn, don't you?"

Turning slightly in my chair, I watched Shelley's face as the woman posed this question. As she continued to pour coffee, Shelley's face remained relatively placid, though I did detect a slight frown before she offered, "I think it's time you take care of yourself, Rose." Then she patted her shoulder before leaving her table, preparing to fill the next patron's cup.

Six months later, Rose's prediction about her boss was right on target. He did marry again, but his bride was not the long-suffering Rose, who had labored for him those past eighteen years. Rather, he married an interior designer—a woman whom he had met only months before on an assignment. I heard Rose resigned from her position while the couple was still honeymooning.

Today, as I sat in my usual corner, A. J. Hastings, a Wall Street powerbroker, pulled his Jaguar into the parking lot. Though he frequented the diner, I was surprised to see him this morning. It was nearly 10 a.m., and it seemed to me he would have empires to create, expand, and destroy by this hour in the morning. As he entered the diner, I could not help but notice he looked a bit piqued. His shoulders seemed stooped, his gait a little slow. "Maybe he's just tired, or maybe I'm a little envious," I thought, recalling his usual proud sauntering while broadcasting his financial coups to anyone who cared to listen.

Today, however, he resembled the hunted, rather than the predator. Before A. J. made his way to his corner table. Shelley was there with his coffee, steaming from his favorite mug, and her customary smile.

"Bet you're surprised to see me at this hour," he said to her.

"Always nice to see you, Mr. Hastings," she answered. "What can I get you?" But A. J. wasn't interested in eating, he seemed to want to talk to her, to justify why he was at the diner at 10 o'clock in the morning.

"You see, I was in the middle of the biggest deal of my life," he explained. "Then the walls caved in, the funding dried up, the backers pulled out." He looked up at her for a second. "Oh, you'd never understand."

Instinctively, Shelley removed the menu, refilled his mug, and patted his shoulder as she moved to the next table. It was evident A. J. needed some time to clear his head.

No more than two minutes later, his solitude came to an abrupt halt. A federal marshal had entered the diner, and was inquiring who owned the black Jag. As I shifted my eyes to the parking lot, I could see a crew had already loaded the car onto a flatbed. A. J.'s head was in his hands, staring into his empty coffee mug, as the marshal approached him.

But Shelley was there first, intercepting him, coffeepot in hand. As she refilled A. J.'s mug, she poured a cup for the marshal. "Can I interest you in today's special?" she asked.

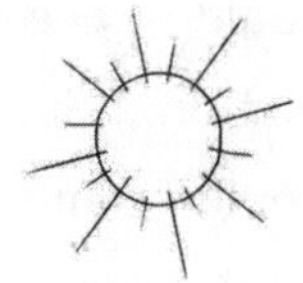

G-O-L-F is a Four-Letter Word

For as long as I can remember, the term golf connoted the worst four-letter word in my vocabulary. As a child, I came to associate the word golf with not having a father. Worse than a jealous mistress, golf had no respect for our family. The pastime consumed all of my father's attention. Weekends, Wednesday afternoons, and holidays would find him fleeing from our home, sporting a guilty countenance. I used to watch him as he loaded his prized collection of clubs into the trunk of our car. The head of each club was lovingly protected by a woolen cover, and I remember thinking that those clubs had more "socks" than my infant brother. His booties rarely matched, and were never as neatly attended to as those golf socks.

As I grew older, my father's obsession with the game became an accepted tradition in our home. If a school play were held on a Wednesday afternoon, I would know that only my mother would be applauding my performance. If a swimming competition were scheduled on a Saturday, I would know that only my mother would be cheering for our team. If a piano recital were scheduled on a Sunday afternoon, I would know only my mother would be subjected to my rendition of *Für Elise.* Other fathers drank beer, watched Monday Night Football, coached Little League; mine played golf.

As a teenager, my father's passion for the game began to irritate me. Those were the days of the early seventies, before superstars like Tiger Woods transformed the game into a chic activity. During this time, I achieved a great deal of satisfaction by poking fun at middle-aged duffers. Those jelly-bellied "athletes," sporting pink shirts and green plaid pants, whiffing their weekends away. It was embarrassing. Images of Neanderthals grasping primitive clubs came to mind, as I spent more civilized weekends reading, writing, and basking in the sun.

At the height of my derision, I felt the ultimate betrayal. My chief accomplice, namely my mother, embraced the game at age forty-five. Tired of being a so-called "golf widow," Mom took to the golf course in style, and within a short time she had mastered the game enough to provide my father with a formidable opponent.

I, on the other hand, remained adamant. Let them make fools of themselves, chasing a tiny ball down numerous fairways. I would have none of it.

As fate would have it, my relationship with the game of golf was about to change. Professionally, I had received a promotion to the director of fundraising at a large urban hospital. Money was desperately needed to purchase cancer equipment, and the board of trustees had had their fill of vendor sales, art auctions, and black-tie dinners. What was needed was something different, something big, something exciting, and something expensive. I shuddered. I could feel it happening—an all-day golf outing was in the works, and I would be responsible for organizing it.

A week into my new job, my worst fear was confirmed. The hospital would sponsor "Links to Health—On Course to Conquer Cancer," with a goal of attracting two hundred golfers and raising $200,000. I was doomed.

During our initial planning meetings, I was astounded at my ignorance of the game of golf. For example, while I knew the difference between a "hook"and a "slice," I had no knowledge of such phrases as "the Callaway system," "Big Berthas,""shotgun starts,"and "Mulligan sales." (When it was suggested to me that additional money could be raised by selling Mulligans, I had originally thought we would need to apply for a temporary liquor license.) During this time, my modus operandi was simple. I kept my mouth shut, took copious notes, and read as much as I could about the dreaded four-letter word—golf.

A month before our outing, I decided to break the news to my father. I could only imagine his reaction. Me, his daughter, was organizing a golf outing! . . . He'd never believe it. He'd probably keel over laughing. However, nothing could have been further from the truth. Upon hearing the news, he seemed rather awestruck, as if I were delivering some sort of beatific message. Then he asked, "What can I do to help?" and "Do you have room for another foursome? I'd like to play."

I was baffled. I just didn't get it. I had graduated from college with honors, obtained a master's degree, secured a management position, married a wonderful man, owned my own home, yet, to my father, nothing seemed to compare to the fact that I was capable of organizing a golf outing.

Over the next four weeks, conversations between my father and me reached a new level of respect for one another. In addition to discussing the upcoming outing, we talked about politics, the stock market, music, literature, and history. For the first time in my life, I felt as if I were just discovering my father, and that dreaded four-letter word was responsible.

The day of the outing dawned rather ominously, with the prediction of thunderstorms. Tee-off time was scheduled at 1 p.m., and by 12:50 p.m., sunlight began streaming through the clouds. I like to think that a Higher Power played a role in that, knowing all the proceeds from the event would be used to help cancer patients. The sunlight continued to hold until the last golfer completed the course. By the time we had gathered in the clubhouse to distribute "Big Berthas" to the winners, a fierce thunderstorm rolled in.

When all was said and done, over two hundred golfers participated in the outing, and over one hundred businesses supported our fundraising journal. Our proceeds totaled an unprecedented $285,000. Six months later, the cancer equipment so desperately needed was purchased, providing hope to those patients diagnosed with the disease.

To this day, I have yet to hold a golf club in my hand, but I view the game differently. Ironically, the very thing I despised most as a child brought me unqualified success as an adult—both as a fundraiser and as a daughter. Yes, golf is still a four-letter word, but so are the words hope and love. And for me, I will forever associate the word golf with hope for cancer patients and love for a father.

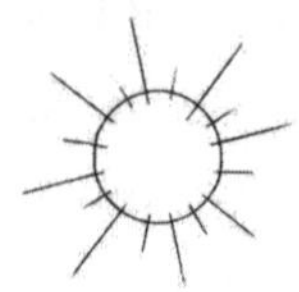

A Poet Lives Here

Barring the first fourteen months of my life, she has been my best friend, my confidante, an extension of myself. We share the same genetics, childhood memories, and parents. So it should come as no surprise that I thought I knew my "little sister" better than anyone else in the world. That is, until the evening of her fortieth birthday.

Traditionally, my sister and I treat each other to a "sisters only" birthday dinner on our special day. After sharing pasta, salad, and wine at our favorite Italian restaurant, I drove her home. That's when she innocently pointed to a gabled stone cottage and sighed, "That has always been my favorite house. Wouldn't it be just heaven to actually live in such a place?"

As she gazed at the home, I heard her sigh. "And that beautiful basket of flowers hanging on the door . . . have you ever seen anything so enchanting? Those flowers actually seem to dance in that basket, don't they?"

Hearing her, I nearly missed the next turn. Not that the house wasn't lovely, but I would never have expected my sister to appreciate it. Did I know her at all? My sister seemed unaffected by both her remark and my reaction, and continued to chatter about her three kids, the crazy dog, her husband's accounting practice. All familiar topics of conversation to me.

As I maneuvered the car into the asphalt driveway of her home, the dog was digging in the lawn, my nephew was bouncing a basketball, my nieces were sitting on the curb, and every light in the house seemed to be burning. Her sports utility vehicle was tethered to the action safely encased in the garage. Life in suburbia at its best.

After a quick hug of thanks, she jumped out of my car and was swallowed up by the domestic chaos that had seemed to define her life for the past seventeen years. As I turned the car around, I backtracked to that quiet street where the stone cottage seemed almost nestled into the landscape. Tranquil, peaceful, so unlike my sister's home. The cobbled driveway curved and flared. A sundial, tucked into a corner of the property, was surrounded by beautiful shrubbery, and a scalloped birdbath offered refreshment for a pair of cardinals. Six graceful gables provided a charming silhouette against the evening sky, and the delicate basket of flowers hanging on the front door provided the finishing touch.

Taking a closer look, I discovered the basket contained at least a dozen silk pansies, and I imagined their yellow and purple heads bending as the door swung open, almost beckoning a welcome to visitors. Looking at the cottage it did seem enchant-ed, and suddenly I felt ashamed of myself. Why wouldn't my sister crave such a tranquil setting? Why had I assumed that her two-story colonial, three rambunctious kids, and an erratic dog were her perception of the American dream?

Oh don't misunderstand me. She'd never forfeit the life she had chosen; she loved her children, her husband, her home, and even that crazy dog, but why wasn't I more in sync with her dreams, her yearnings, and inspirations? I remembered her as a young teen; she shunned typical novels and romances, preferring to spend her time reading poetry and clipping quotations. I thought perhaps someday she would write her own volume of reflec-tions. Where was that precocious young woman? Did she get lost somewhere between motherhood and her fortieth birthday?

The following day, I stopped at a local florist. Selecting a delicate basket from one of the displays, I said, "I'd like you to fill this with silk pansies, purple and yellow, to be exact. The flowers need to be arranged as artistically as possible. You see, it's for the front door of a very special home."

The florist smiled at me. "I think I understand. You'd like the basket to hold, shall we say, a floral welcome wagon. I can arrange the flowers so their petals almost nod whenever the door is opened. Is that what you'd like?"

I looked at the florist in amazement. "That's exactly what I want. But how did you know?"

"Because I completed a similar basket recently," he said. "This one must be for a special person, as well. Tell me, is it for a painter or a musician? Only a creative type would be sensitive enough to order such a piece."

"Actually it's for a poet," I responded. "And you can expect her first work to be published very soon."

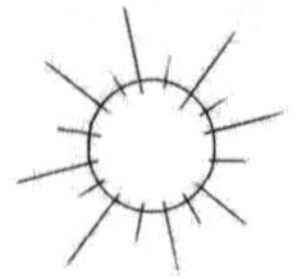

A Life's Lesson on a Mountaintop

When most people think of Switzerland, images of rich choco-lates, cuckoo clocks, and majestic mountains probably come to mind. However, whenever I reminisce about that beautiful Alpine country, my thoughts turn to a wizened old man with a paralyzed limb, and eyes that could only be described as robin's egg blue.

Twenty-five years ago I visited Switzerland as a senior in high school. Though I always promised myself to return to that Tyrolean landscape, I have yet to honor that vow. And while that trip instilled in me a sincere appreciation of natural beauty, it also provided me with a deeper insight into the human spirit.

I still remember it was very early on a Sunday morning. My classmates and I had spent the previous evening at several bier-gartens, laughing, singing, and yes, imbibing a bit with the delightful Swiss. Having drifted in rather early Sunday morn-ing, no one seemed overly concerned about attending church services. No one, that is, except me.

Feeling quite virtuous, I rose, washed, and quickly dressed in the early dawn. As I left our hotel, I remembered the nearest church was located about midway up a slight hill. Locating the path, I looked up. The hill suddenly seemed more like a mountain, and I tentatively started my climb. As I negotiated the rather difficult path, I could not help thinking I was a particularly good person. Rather smugly, I silently gave myself that proverbial pat on the back.

I thought to myself, "Here I am making my way through an obstacle course in the cold, gray dawn, while my classmates are still sleeping soundly in the warm comfort of our hotel. Aren't I quite noble?" I could not help but feel quite proud of myself.

Within about twenty-five yards of the church, my eyes focused on a image I shall never forget. Making his way slowly down the mountain was a wizened, elderly man. Crippled with arthritis, he moved with the utmost care. One of his gnarled hands was clenched over a makeshift cane. Very deliberately, he placed the walking stick before him, taking extra time to steady it. Then, very slowly he advanced one leg. Taking time to get his bearings, he continued to persevere, dragging a paralyzed leg behind him.

Reaching the church door first, I held it open for him. He looked up at me with the most beautiful eyes I had ever seen—an azure blue that seemed almost supernatural against the gray morning light. "His are not ordinary eyes," I remember thinking. "These are eyes that can see the beauty in a cold morning, dignity in a crippled body, and grace in a torturous mountain path. These are the eyes that reflect the essence of one's very soul."

"Dankeschoen, Fraulein," he smiled at me, as we entered the church together, "aren't we blessed to be able to visit the Lord this morning?"

And, suddenly, I was ashamed. "Ah, but Fraulein," he continued, "your path was much more difficult than mine. I had only to make my way down the mountain."

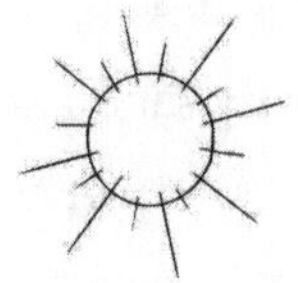

WISDOM AT THE WATER'S EDGE

The summer I turned twelve had every indication of becoming the lowest point in my young life. However, thanks to the wisdom of a dear aunt, and the beauty of a natural wonder, that particular summer provided me with a deep strength I have drawn upon throughout my life.

Earlier that year, my parents had decided to end their fifteen-year marriage. The only home I had ever known would be sold, life with my father would be reduced to a weekend experience, and I would begin seventh grade in a new school. While all of these changes were terrifying to me, somehow that June they didn't seem to matter that much. What disturbed me the most was foregoing our annual vacation in the mountains. Instead of spending the summer tucked away in the cool, verdant forest, I was going to spend the next ten weeks with my elderly aunt, who lived in a quiet seashore community. From what little I knew, the only friends I could expect to make were seagulls.

Needless to say, I did not want to go. I had never been a fan of gritty sand and salty surf, and though I did love my aunt, I hadn't seen her in nine years. I barely remembered her and I sincerely doubted she would be much of a companion to me. But I had no choice in the matter. My parents were breaking up, not only with each other, but also our home. The only thing they agreed upon that summer was removing me from the battlefield.

So despite my misgivings and protests, the very day school closed I found myself sitting on a train heading south. Beside me were two canvas bags that held my summer clothes, my books, and a daily journal I had been keeping since learning of my parents' impending divorce. Traveling with me, too, was a heart so heavy with resentment, bitterness, and loss, I found it difficult to breathe.

When the train pulled into the station, I was the last passenger to leave my seat. The conductor must have sensed how desperate I felt because he patted my shoulder as if to offer assurance that things would somehow sort themselves out. But I knew better, for my life would never be the same.

Waiting for me on the platform was Aunt Olivia, who was actually my grandmother's eldest sister. Demure, slender, and almost shy, she smiled at me, then hesitantly patted my shoulder, in much the same manner as the conductor. I suppose I must have looked as forlorn to her as I had to him.

Poor Olivia, I thought. She was as much a victim as I in this desperate situation. Her summer plans had not included a ten-week visit from a grandniece. I tried to force a smile for her, and I remember thinking how out of place she seemed at the station, almost like a young girl dressed up in her mother's clothes. I was suddenly reminded of an old *Highlights* magazine from my childhood. Its theme was "what doesn't belong,"and even to the most casual observer, Aunt Olivia seemed almost foreign standing in that station—like a baby seagull confined in a birdcage.

Hauling my canvas bags in the direction of the taxi stand, I trudged after Aunt Olivia, who moved with surprising grace and speed for an older woman. Fortunately, the line was a short one and Aunt Olivia and I were soon seated in an old-fashioned taxi cab heading east toward the shoreline. In no time at all, the landscape started to change. With my face pressed against the window, I noticed the city with its tall buildings, traffic, and people soon receded. Within a half hour I sensed a hint of salty air and viewed a series of ramshackle bungalows bearing signs like "Bait and Tackle,""The Chowder Shack,"and "Boating Supplies."

Three blocks from the ocean, Aunt Olivia directed the driver to stop in front of a small, pink cottage. As I dragged my bags up the seashell path to the front door, I remember thinking the house looked like Cinderella's coach, a transformed pumpkin. I tried to swallow the lump that was forming in my throat as I thought, this will be my home for the next ten weeks.

Settling in with Aunt Olivia was much easier than I had anticipated. To her credit, she respected my privacy and sensed my need to be left alone. She didn't try to distract me with useless activities or engage me in meaningless chatter. Because the cottage was so tiny, my aunt had adopted a very simple lifestyle, which, looking back, was precisely what I needed at the time. Since the dwelling was so small, I slept in an open loft, tucked in the eaves. Every night, as I climbed the ladder to my bedroom in the stars, I felt like Heidi. But unlike my storybook heroine, I had a view of the ocean, not the mountains that were so familiar to me.

During the day, I used a rusty bicycle that had once belonged to my mother to travel. For the first few days, I purposely avoided the ocean and beach, preferring to exhaust myself pedaling alone into town. At the time I didn't think that much about it, but in retrospect I think there was so much anger in me I was unable to even see, much less appreciate, the beauty of the shoreline.

By the fourth morning, I somehow found myself pedaling to the beach. It was a beautiful clear sunrise, and while I had always been partial to the mountains, the seascape before me held a unique beauty. When I arrived at the beach, it was virtually empty, but for two lone silhouettes—one feeding the seagulls, the other fortifying a sand castle against the approaching tide.

Leaving my bike on the boardwalk, I ventured toward the sea. As I walked, I studied the figure feeding the gulls. There was something vaguely familiar about the stance. A natural grace, the fluid movements, almost an affinity with the sea. Then it hit me—it was Aunt Olivia. Dressed in worn jeans, a faded T-shirt, and a baseball cap, she resembled a young teenager from a distance. I remembered the dichotomy of seeing her in the train station, stressed, strained, and out of place. Here, against the backdrop of the sea, pounding surf, and beach, she was home.

Though she did not turn toward me, she sensed my presence. "Have some bread," she said softly, handing me some crusts without taking her eyes off the pair of gulls she was feeding. As I crumbled the crusts, the sound of the gulls overhead, the scent of the salty air, and the sight of the young boy defending his sand castle effected a calmness within me. I had not felt such peace since learning of my parents' impending divorce.

Long after the last of the bread was gone, Aunt Olivia and I continued to watch the boy. Finally, she spoke, "You have to admire the persistence in that boy," she said softly. "He's trying so hard to defend that castle. He's decorated it with beautiful shells, he's put his heart and soul into that project. But no matter how high the walls or how deep the moat he builds, the ocean is stronger and more powerful."

As she spoke, I watched the boy. The closer the tide came, the more frenzied he became. His digging became manic, his face was marked with apprehension at each wave. Finally, Aunt Olivia extended her hand to me and, together, we walked down to the water's edge.

The boy looked up at us. At first, he seemed confused, but then I saw him smile. Aunt Olivia must have extended her other hand because the boy left his sand castle, stood up, and took her hand. As the three of us watched, a final wave crashed upon the castle, leveling it to the sand, destroying the walls, and flooding the moat.

As the seashells that had decorated the castle were scattered, Aunt Olivia released our hands. "Let's collect as many of these beautiful shells as we can," she said. "These shells were actually the best part of that castle. Let's gather them together. We'll use them to build a new castle in a more protected area." And that's just what we did.

Throughout my life, Aunt Olivia's words have guided me on more occasions than I care to remember. That day on the beach would help me countless times as I fought to rebuild my life after forces beyond my control sent me into a tailspin. Years later, as I struggled to survive my own divorce, a corporate downsizing, and the death of a best friend, Aunt Olivia's soft words would quiet my heart. And while attempting to rebuild my life, I tried to follow Aunt Olivia's example by taking the best of my previous existence with me, to ensure that each new castle I erected was a little bit better, a little bit richer, and a little bit stronger than the one before.

This story was originally published in *Whispers from Heaven Magazine*, Summer 2000.

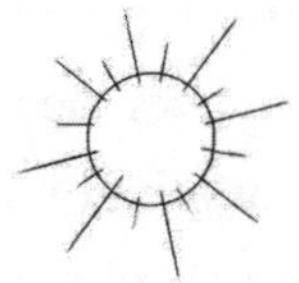

NAILING DOWN A DREAM

The outrageously funny comedienne, Gilda Radner, once said, "I base my fashion taste on what doesn't itch . . ." and sitting in a posh nail salon, I had to smile. Gazing out the shop's front window, I lifted my eyes to the heavens and winked at the sky. "Truer words have never been spoken, Gilda," I whispered to her.

I looked down at my hands, and studied my fingernails—my reason for being here. Short, bluntly filed with clear no-nonsense polish, they looked perfect under the nail dryer. With a daily work schedule that included eight hours of banging on a computer keyboard, I estimated their lifespan of perfection would last approximately seven minutes.

Having headed up the public relations function at a large urban hospital for over a decade now, I had promised myself this past New Year's Eve to schedule a weekly manicure. While seeing my young assistants sporting acrylic wraps and seasonal decals did little to encourage me in honoring this resolution, young Kim Loo, the beautiful Korean nail technician, managed to perform minor miracles on my hands. In two weeks I was hooked. Clean and simple, like Eddie Bauer and J. Crew, nothing dramatic, nothing itchy, Gilda would have applauded.

While I basked in the end result of this process, the most tedious task was sitting still, with fingers splayed, under the nail dryer. Initially, my eyes were riveted on the tiny hourglass that was placed near the drying area for clients like myself who seemed to develop a sudden attention deficit disorder. After several seconds of watching the pink sand travel from one glass partition to another, I found the hourglass did little to relieve my boredom.

At that point I began to surreptitiously study the other women in the salon. While it certainly did not compare to an outdoor cafe situated on the left bank of Paris, I discovered I had an orchestra seat, center aisle in people-watching.

During the next few weeks, I had become an expert in what I had redefined as nail-watching. Clients were basically divided into five categories: the twenty-something party animals, who needed the latest, craziest fads; the career types, who needed to portray a corporate image; the stay-at-home moms, who needed some pampering; the full-time moms, part-time workers, who needed all of the above; and the older women, who would rather visit the salon for professional services than their own podiatrists.

As the weeks progressed, I passed the time under the nail dryer by mentally categorizing the various clients. While most of the women were relatively easy to classify, such as the corporate climber sporting a French manicure, the older woman showing off her ringed fingers with a "Pretty in Pink" backdrop, or the twenty-something fanning acrylic wraps painted blue, there was one woman who defied all of my classifications.

Dressed in some sort of a brown uniform, consisting of roomy trousers, a baggy shirt, and unlaced work boots, she seemed so out of place. Glancing at her, I could not help but think of a wild bird confined to a cage—perhaps a spacious one, but a wired prison, all the same. Her nails, too, were another dichotomy. Looking at them reminded me of the flaming red talons of a hawk.

But the woman to whom they belonged seemed anything but predatory. Rather her long, heavy mane of hair was streaked with gray, and pulled into a too-tight braid. Her full face, devoid of cosmetics, looked so innocent and open. But studying her more closely, I thought I could detect some sadness in her eyes.

I thought about that woman often during the following weeks. There was something familiar about her, though I could not determine what. Was she a former teacher, athletic coach, or neighbor? As luck would have it, our nail-drying time soon overlapped, and I found myself seated across from the woman. Wanting to break the ice, I smiled at her and told her I liked the color she had selected. Thankfully, on that particular day, her nails were painted a pale pink, rather than a neon orange. She noticeably blushed, as she looked down at her hands, and seemed to nod.

"Yes, this color is more like me,"she considered carefully. It was at that moment I realized why she looked so familiar to me. A child of the 1970s, I had grown up listening to Carol King. Looking at this woman, I realized if she freed her hair from that braid, replaced her brown attire with a free-flowing gown, and declawed her fingernails, she could have posed for the cover of the "Tapestry"album.

Before thinking that I might offend her, I blurted out, "Has anyone ever told you that you look like Carol King?" When she did not respond, I asked her, "Are you a musician, an artist?"

At first I thought I must have overstepped my bounds, but when I looked at her, her eyes were brimming with tears, and she finally said, "That's the nicest thing anyone has said to me for such a long time. I used to be an artist, a sculptor. I used to love working with my hands, sinking them into wet clay, and creating something beautiful, but that was a long time ago."

"You know, you do have the hands of an artist," I told her.

Looking down at her hands, she said, "But these fake fingernails really don't fit, do they?"

Not trusting myself to speak, I remained silent.

"I had a terrible experience,"she continued. "Someone stole all my work, my ideas, I lost everything . . . that's when I gave up. I just quit. I got a regular job. I'm still at a museum, but I work in the maintenance department. I keep the gallery areas clean.

The pay's okay, the benefits are good, and I can still be close to the things I love . . ."

Listening to her rationalizations, I wanted to add, "And just to ensure you would never be tempted to sculpt anything again, never be tempted into sinking your hands into that clay you love so much, you continue these weekly visits to this salon."

Thinking of all the talent she had locked away in those beautiful hands, I wanted to scream, "Why must you mutilate your gifted fingers every week by confining them to a prison of artificial plastics in the form of wraps and tips," but I remained silent.

Finally, I swallowed hard, and smiled at her. "That's so peculiar. I never would have pegged you for a maintenance engineer. A sculptor? Yes. A musician? Yes. But a person in plant operations? No way! I am sorry, but I just don't see it."

Suddenly aware of her need to be left alone, I smiled again, patted her shoulder, and left the salon. Later that same afternoon I'm told, Kim Loo was requested to remove all ten artificial nails from a Carol King look-alike, whose only explanation was a sudden career change. And since that afternoon, I myself have been religiously reading the museum's newsletter for any information concerning a new sculpture exhibit. I sense a rave review in the making.

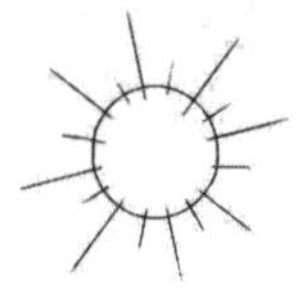

GROVER CLEVELAND
SLEPT HERE

When my fifty-year-old husband made a conscious decision to leave the proverbial corporate rat race behind and take another position in a local college, I was his staunchest supporter. True, the salary would be a bit less, the benefits package not as rich, and the prestige somewhat diminished, but the real payoff would come with less stress, a reduced commute, and more time off. Or so I thought . . .

The truth is, while he logged fewer hours with the college, the time he did work seemed to overlap considerably with our sacrosanct weekends, which had always been a precious commodity. Having never had children, my husband and I had developed a special camaraderie through the years. Rather than attending dance recitals, soccer games, or school plays, we spent our weekends browsing through antique shops, visiting bookstores, and sipping cappuccino. To the casual observer saddled with child-rearing responsibilities, this may seem like an idyllic existence.

However, a childless marriage does have its share of heartbreak. Holidays like Christmas, Mother's Day, and Father's Day can be especially cruel. To compensate, we made a special effort to indulge ourselves in simple pleasures during the weekends, which made my husband's new schedule especially difficult for me.

By his second month with the college, I knew I would need to rearrange my own weekend schedule—particularly Saturday afternoons—if our marriage were not to be adversely affected. Not being the type to frequent shopping malls, nor one to have a fetish for fashions or furnishings, I tried to diligently plan my new-found time with the utmost care and thought. If I were losing my "best friend" every Saturday, the least I could do was arrange an enjoyable activity for my solo excursions!

Being confined to an office setting during the week, I decided to incorporate exercise into my routine, so walking became my transportation of choice. Fortunately, we live in a pretty suburban area, surrounded by history. So, donning a sturdy pair of walking shoes, I set off, prepared to explore my hometown and the neighboring community.

During my first excursion, I decided to walk the two-mile trek down Bloomfield Avenue, which serves as the main street of our town. My initial discovery was that storefronts, homes, and restaurants look different when one passes them on foot, rather than cruising by in a motorized vehicle. Colors, textures, shapes and sizes become more vibrant, more distinct. Then I began to take notice of things that had previously escaped me—beautiful window boxes bursting with flowers, a new shop specializing in international coffees, a tiny ice cream parlor serving gourmet flavors. During my walk, I popped into each of these establishments to browse and chat with their proprietors.

After exploring the nooks and crannies of my own town, I headed west to discover the treasures of the neighboring one. The following week, I passed a beautiful, well-tended clapboard colonial home, which was maintained by the National Department of Parks. Though a handsome sign named the landmark, I needed no such assistance. It was the birthplace of Grover Cleveland, the twenty-second and twenty-fourth president of the United States. During the past twenty years, I had passed the home countless times, never venturing inside. Today, however, would be different, I thought as I crossed the manicured lawn, and climbed the steps leading to the front door.

My knock was answered by an attractive woman whose personal history I was easily as intrigued by as the house itself. "I am your guide, and it's a pleasure to welcome you to the birthplace of Stephen Grover Cleveland," she said.

"I never knew his name was Stephen," I responded.

"No one does," she answered. "In fact, I think that was a question on *Jeopardy* and nobody got it right. Come in and pay a visit to the nineteenth century."

For the next forty minutes, I was enlightened about the life and times of "Stephen" Grover Cleveland. I learned he was born in 1837 in a decidedly middle-class house, located across the street from the First Presbyterian Church, where his father had served as minister. In a whimsical fashion, she explained that Grover Cleveland was a bachelor when he assumed the presidency in 1885, and made history one year later by becoming the first president to marry in the White House. His wife, Frances Clara Folsom, was twenty-seven years his junior, and was the daughter of his law firm partner.

I learned the Clevelands had five children, and their first-born, Ruth, had a candy bar named for her. Their second child, Esther, had her own claim in history. She was the first baby of a president to be born in the White House.

Politically, I learned that Cleveland served as mayor of Buffalo, governor of New York, and was the only Democrat elected president between 1861 and 1912. As for his two non-consecutive terms as president, I was informed that although he won the popular vote in his 1888 reelection bid, he lost the electoral vote. After the defeat, as the Clevelands were packing their belongings to move from the White House, Mrs. Cleveland told the heartbroken staff, "Don't worry, we'll be back in four years," and in 1892, they returned.

But as fascinated as I was with the Clevelands, my personal guide intrigued me even more. Listening to her, I could readily appreciate her enthusiasm for our twenty-second and twenty-fourth president. Yet, she did not strike me as an historical buff or a museum curator. Somehow, I envisioned her to be more at home in the "great outdoors," rather than tucked away in memorabilia of the nineteenth century.

At the conclusion of the tour, I complimented her on her knowledge and presentation skills, and asked her how she managed to find herself as the Cleveland spokesperson. She laughed, and told me she was probably the most unlikely candidate. "As a student, I actually hated history," she said. "At that time, I could not be bothered memorizing dates and events because I knew I would never use the information. In fact, I even challenged my history teacher with that line of reasoning."

She continued, "I always loved being outside, so when I graduated, I got a job with the parks department on a reservation, not too far from here."

After working there several years, she explained, this position opened up. During the interview, she was asked what she knew about Grover Cleveland. "I didn't even know he had been a president," she told me.

"Well, you certainly were a quick study," I said with a smile as I left.

In the coming weeks, I thought a lot about her as I continued my "solo Saturdays." While she certainly had enlightened me about Grover Cleveland, she taught me a more important, universal principle. Sometimes, what we may dismiss as stupid, needless, or frivolous at the time, may just turn out to be an important cornerstone in our lives.

And somehow I think history teachers everywhere may agree...

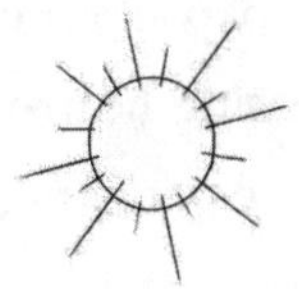

CHRISTMAS IN JULY

When people brag about the lucrative bonuses, fabulous perks, and rich stock options their careers offer, I usually feign a mild interest and listen. Then predictably, I hear about 401(k)s that are matched dollar for dollar, benefit plans that underwrite the family pet, and company stock that has quadrupled over the past six months. Invariably, I smile, murmur something polite, and change the subject to the current weather pattern.

While the poor urban hospital for which I work offers none of the above, I feel that I have been blessed more than my corporate counterparts could ever imagine. But not in monetary terms, rather with a dedicated, caring, and loving staff. The four of us have been together for nearly fifteen years, and we undoubtedly know more about each other than our own families know about us. And I have learned more about myself merely by being with them.

Perhaps it is because we have spent so much time together, witnessing heart-warming triumphs, as well as weathering heart-wrenching tragedies. Working side-by-side in life-and-death situations has a way of catapulting you into each others' souls. There is neither the time nor the luxury of slowly progressing from a polite "nodding acquaintance" when someone's life is hanging in the balance.

That's why when our birthdays roll around, I try to devote as much time to selecting the perfect card, ordering the most delicious cake, and selecting the most appropriate gift as I do with my own family—for they, my coworkers, are truly just as treasured.

Naively, I thought I had known nearly all there was to learn about them until Audrey, the most quiet and introverted member of our department celebrated her fifty-first birthday. In keeping with her demure nature, I had selected, as in past years, a birthday card depicting a cascading waterfall with an inspirational quotation by Ralph Waldo Emerson. Tucked inside the card were tickets to the Botanical Gardens, a bucolic retreat located about ten miles away. Audrey seemed very pleased, and displayed the card on her desk.

During the course of the day I happened to bump into Joanie, our office clown, at the copy machine. In her hand was Audrey's birthday card. "I just had to make a copy of this," she told me, pointing to the quotation on the card. "The words are the most beautiful ones I have ever read. I want to post them over my desk."

I was dumbfounded. For fifteen years I had been foraging the card stores to find the perfect comical birthday greeting for Joanie, complete with cartoon figures and nonsensical verse. And little did I ever imagine that Ralph Waldo Emerson had made her heart sing. How cavalier of me to think I knew her so well!

When Joanie's birthday approached, I ditched my regular routine of combing through the racks of comic cards, and headed to those with inspirational words. Then, instead of enclosing the typical gift certificate to her favorite department store, I bought her an aromatic candle, a blank journal book, and a meditation cassette tape. During the next few months, I knew she replaced the candle twice, and sometimes during the day, I happened to "catch" her furtively scribbling some soul-searching words in her journal. As for the tape, she told me it was nearly worn out from constant use. I was amazed.

With her flaming red hair, Eileen was our departmental manager, and like so many of her ancestors, she shared a delightful wit, quick temper, and the proverbial "Irish stomach." She was loath to experiment in the gastrometric field, and meat and potatoes were her constant food fare. When her birthday rolled around again, I decided to try something different. Originally, I had been entertaining the idea of spending her birthday at a sushi bar, but reconsidered. We needed to take smaller steps.

So we decided on a Thai restaurant that had recently opened in the downtown area. While I cannot say Eileen would not have preferred an Irish pub, we shared so many laughs over the menu that I doubt our enjoyment could have been replicated over beer and burgers. The food was an adventure in itself for our birthday girl, as she discovered the pleasures of sweetened Thai tea, coconut shrimp, and fresh oranges drizzled in chocolate.

A July baby, I had always prided myself that my birthday was the most distanced, calendar-wise, from the crazy Christmas season—and I liked that! While the spirit of the holiday continued to stir my soul, I would find the commercial hustle and bustle, like the cold, dreary days of December, was becoming more of a burden. In direct contrast was my July birthday. The simplicity of a sunny day, the joy of summer clothing, and a slice of angel food cake topped with a small dollop of cream and fresh strawberries was delightful.

Entering my office on the morning of my birthday, it was difficult to find my desk. Garnished with holiday decorations, including a pink aluminum Christmas tree and a huge plastic Santa, my office had been transformed into the worst "Christmas in July" nightmare I had ever witnessed. I doubled over laughing. My birthday, a day reserved for quiet reflection, personal evaluation, and meditative introspection, had been infiltrated by multi-colored blinking lights, a noxious-smelling pine candle, and the Chipmunks blaring carols overhead. Appropriately, my birthday cake was a frozen Yule log, garishly decorated with plastic sprigs of holly and a team of reindeer.

Ironically, that birthday celebration changed my life forever. Six months later, Christmas was the most peaceful, most spiritual I had ever experienced. Perhaps I needed to see those commercial trappings of the holiday in somewhat of a distorted manner.

Maybe, I needed to view them out-of-season, against the back-drop of a hot July morning to eradicate them from my life.

Perhaps it was the only way I could truly appreciate the price of that excess, and how I was ransoming my soul every Christmas.

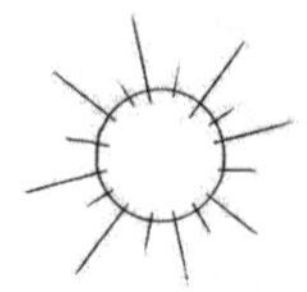

You Have Mail

Like most people, I enjoy hearing from family and friends, and one of the most rewarding aspects of subscribing to America Online, or AOL, for me, is clicking on that familiar icon when it informs me, "You Have Mail." But unlike most, I imagine the mail has a special significance for me as one of the most important people I have ever known, my dear grandfather, spent a lifetime sorting, stamping, weighing, and delivering mail.

Accessing my electronic mail, I thought for the umpteenth time I wish that Grandpa could have lived long enough to experience the wonders of the Internet. Greetings from my niece in New England, a cousin in Japan, and a college friend in South America were waiting to be read. As I scanned their words on the screen, my thoughts kept returning to Grandpa. In my mind's eye, I saw him standing behind the counter of the local postal branch, green visor in place, shirt sleeves rolled to the elbows, diligently taking care of the postal needs of his various patrons.

"We need to add the ZIP code for Boston," he'd say, looking up the five-digit code. "A one-ounce letter to Japan has gone up ten cents," he'd inform another. "Air mail to South America is now only four days," he'd tell a third, as he proudly attached the "Par Avion" stickers to the envelope. Beginning his career with the United States Post Office in 1915, I asked myself, could he ever have conceived the wonders of an instantaneous click of a mouse?

Or the power of a chat room? While I, as a forty-something baby boomer, still had a difficult time appreciating the phenomenal appeal this activity seemed to generate, I imagine my grandfather would have been completely bewildered. As a letter carrier, his route consisted of scores of houses, businesses, and factories. All were inhabited by real people—homemakers, employees, children, retirees. While he delivered the mail, he chatted frequently with all of them, taking time to share a cup of tea or coffee, or a slice of pie. He met them face-to-face, eye-to-eye. He knew their names, where they lived, and probably more about their personal histories and intimacies than other members of their very own families.

I suppose that delivering letters through two world wars, carrying certified mail for over three decades, and bringing long-awaited news from inside the Iron Curtain, tended to make him more of a surrogate family member. Pondering over those relationships he had forged through the years, I cannot help but think he'd have little respect for the appeal of a bantering anonymous chat room. And what of the "instant translation" services now available? He would have marveled at that state-of-the-art technology! In our small northern New Jersey neighborhoods, he had played an important role with each new wave of immigration. In the very beginning, I wonder if he was apprehensive or even ashamed of his Irish brogue as he delivered mail to the White, Anglo-Saxon, Protestant residents which inhabited the majority of the homes on his route. At the time, his fellow brethren in Boston were being told they "need not apply" for any available work.

The "waspy" neighborhoods of the early 1900s soon grew to embrace the newcomers from Germany, Ireland, Poland, and Italy, and Grandpa would be only too happy to assist these new Americans address a letter to the "old country." His translation services were, no doubt, neither as instantaneous nor as accurate as those delivered by the various Internet providers, but they were given freely with personal empathy and concern. In turn, his personal services were rewarded in kind with homemade strudel, soda bread, kielbasa, and pastry, rather than a monthly subscriber fee.

But even during Grandpa's career with the United States Post Office, technology was changing the landscape. I can still remember his reaction when the Post Office introduced the Zone Improvement Plan (ZIP) code project in 1963. In a single word, Grandpa was horrified. In his mind, it was inconceivable that the government would assign a numerical system to manage such a personal task as delivering the mail. Nevertheless, though he personally objected to the new ZIP code system, he was a good soldier. In fact, he was one of the selected few chosen to promote ZIP codes to businesses and corporations throughout the state.

At the time, corporate America was using addressograph

machines to produce their mailing materials. Names and addresses were imprinted upon metal plates which were then inked and pressed to blank envelopes or labels. Business leaders objected vehemently to the cost of producing all new plates to incorporate the new ZIP code on the addresses. Poor Grandpa would have to travel throughout the state with his numerous charts and graphs that had divided the country into various sections, subsections, states, counties, and towns. During his presentations, he was obligated to preach the merits of the ZIP code project, with a hokey slogan that translated something like, "Remember ZIP moves the mail, and mail moves the country... Do your part. Use ZIP codes!"

Though he had never personally endorsed the new system, I know he felt a sense of pride when it became fully operational, as he had played a tangible role in its success. Years later, when the ZIP+4 system was introduced, I know Grandpa thought the government had pushed the proverbial (mailing) envelope too far. Fortunately, he had already retired by that time. A veteran of the U.S. Postal Service, he had fought and won the War of the Five Digit ZIP Code. To increase this code to nine numbers in his mind was totally ridiculous. I remember him scoffing, "And this they call progress?"

As I turned my attention back to my computer screen, I smiled again thinking of my grandfather's outrage with the ZIP+4 system. What would he have ever thought about E-mail? But then, I considered carefully, he just may have thought E-mail was a feat to be applauded. After all, what seems easier to remember and more personal? Mail from UncleSam@usa.gov or a letter from

Barbara Davey

20515-9995 (the ZIP+4 address for the Postal Office in Washington, DC)?

And then I imagined that somewhere in cyberspace, there just may be an elderly gentleman wearing a green visor, shirt sleeves rolled to the elbows, overseeing the world's E-mail. And I think I can hear him applauding.

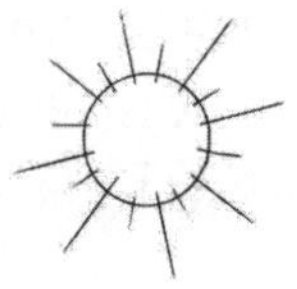

Upon Reaching the Shoreline

From my earliest recollection, I have always had a deep fascination with the ocean. While other bodies of water, such as rivers, lakes, and streams, have their unique appeal, nothing has ever captivated my attention and admiration as much as the vast, infinite, timeless beauty of the Atlantic. Perhaps it was because my childhood summers were spent at the Jersey shore, and the ocean played an essential role in making every vacation so memorable. But, somehow, I have an inkling that even if my earliest summer holidays were spent in a lakefront cottage or in a mountain retreat, my heart would have found its way back to the ocean.

As a child, I remember writing messages on sheets of parchment paper, rolling them up, and inserting them into glass bottles. Corking the tops, I would wade into the water at low tide and set my memoirs floating. I trusted the ocean to carry them off to Ireland, my mother's homeland. To the best of my knowledge, none of them ever made their way across the Atlantic.

Sometimes I would discover the bottles, still corked, a few days later, washed upon the shoreline, a quarter of a mile south of where I had launched them.

Perhaps because of its vastness and its unpredictability, my fascination with the ocean included a morbid side as well. In my mind, while nothing could compare to its beauty on a clear, calm July afternoon, I was also familiar with its horrific side. As a child, I remember thinking how the ocean was somehow responsible for countless disasters, including the ill-fated Titanic. I recalled how the ocean acted as a perfect camouflage for such lethal enemies as sharks and submarines, and how it was capable of merely "swallowing" downed airplanes and crippled ocean liners.

But to me, it was also the most magnificent of all creations. It served as a natural habitat of my favorite childhood animal, the gray whale, and was home to my imaginary friend, the mermaid. Years later, in a fifth grade science class, when I learned that the earliest life forms originated in the ocean, I was not surprised. I think I had always known that in my heart, but I just needed the time to have my mind and science confirm it.

One of the greatest thrills I had as a child was experiencing the ocean firsthand. Observing youngsters today, I know I was not unique in this pursuit. How often have children run down to the beach, merely pausing to throw their towels on the sand, and then dash into the water? I was no different.

As many other beaches with ocean swimming, ours had its

swimming areas clearly defined. Banked by the shoreline, three ropes, secured by bright red buoys, delineated a large, rectangular area which was restricted for swimming. Four lifeguards diligently safeguarded the area, and all of us respected the boundaries. In fact, the buoyed ropes had made such an impression on me that staying "inside the ropes" became somewhat of a universal truth. Absolutes such as "a square must have four equal sides . . . a circle must have 360 degrees . . . swimmers must stay inside the ropes" dictated my childhood.

In addition to delineating the swimming area, the ropes also served an important recreational purpose. For years, I remember my grandparents and countless other "grown-ups" in my life would venture into the ocean holding onto the ropes and letting the waves roll over them. During high tide, the buoys would serve as a primitive floatation device. Thinking back, I doubt many of these adults had mastered the art of swimming, and these ropes probably boosted their confidence in the water, in addition to confining them into a concentrated area for their own protection.

Or so I believed, until an experience at age ten changed my way of thinking about those ropes forever. Early that morning, I was one of the first people to arrive at the beach. As most ten-year-olds, I wasted no time in racing into the water. Though I was never athletic, I had always excelled in water sports, and I was a fairly strong swimmer. As I began my crawl stroke to the further buoy, I sensed something was amiss—something did not feel quite right. I seemed to be swimming at a peculiar angle, and, even at ten, I knew something was very wrong with the water.

I wasted no time floating by the distant buoys. I wanted to return to shore, so I started swimming back. Instead of heading to the beach, however, I kept turning sideways, and continued to bump against the buoys, each time becoming entangled in the ropes. Every time I tried to push away, kicking with all of my might, the water carried me back.

For the first time in my life, I remember panicking, as every morbid aspect of my beautiful ocean played through my mind. Images of the shipwrecks, the downed planes, the hungry sharks, and the horrible drownings became so real to me. I could actually see the terror in every victim of each scenario as I prepared myself to become another tragic statistic as well.

How long I struggled I could not gauge. Looking back it was probably less than two minutes, though I had experienced what seemed to be a lifetime of distress. I suddenly became aware of a lifeguard's presence, and I remember him saying to me, "Things are okay. I'm right here. You need to go under the rope, and we'll swim back to shore together."

Even in my terror, I remember saying to him, "But you can't do that. You always have to stay inside the ropes."

"Not always," he answered, lifting the rope. "Come on," and both of us ducked under, and swam on a long diagonal angle to shore. Like my corked bottles, we ended up nearly a quarter of a mile south from where we had entered, and we walked back in the early morning sun. Because the currents were so strong that day, all swimming was prohibited, and we children amused ourselves at the water's edge building sand castles.

Later that afternoon, I remember the lifeguard drew a diagram in the sand for me, and explained how the effect of the strong undertow made it impossible for me to swim to shore in a straight line. "That's why we had to go outside the ropes and around the current. It was the only way to get back. "

Though I was appreciative of his explanation, I had learned a more important lesson that day which went beyond currents, undertows, and angles. Though I was still too young to grasp all of its implications, I would recall this experience often throughout my life. At times, just as the ocean would not be governed by such restrictions as buoyed ropes, so in life, I had begun to sense, I would sometimes need to bend or break the rules to be true to myself and my core beliefs.

And, like my long diagonal swim, the journey may be tedious and frightening, but sometimes that may be the only way to reach the shoreline of our dreams.

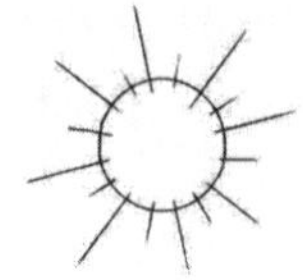

—*Hebrews 13:1*

STICKLER IS A GOOD NAME FOR A CANCER CENTER

Locking up my office for the night, I glanced out the window at the gray sky and sleeting rain. Cold, wintry nights in January were certainly not among my favorite things. I longed for the comfort of my warm home, worn sweat suit and a steaming cup of soup, but I had one last stop to make before heading out. Little did I realize at the time, it would probably be the most significant detour I would make in my entire life.

For the past twelve years, I had been employed by an urban hospital as the director of marketing and public relations. Just recently, with the cutbacks in healthcare, my responsibilities had been expanded to include fundraising—with no additional salary or staff. Nevertheless, I was committed to my new job description. Earlier that day, I had been summoned by the head nurse on the oncology unit. One of her patients had asked to meet "the person in charge of raising money."

As I entered the patient's room, the nurse's words echoed in my mind. "Her name is Sarah Stickler, and she's quite an eccentric. I don't know what to make of her. Actually, nobody does. She looks like a street person; in fact, some of the nurses are taking up a collection for her. She needs clothing, food, and dental work, but then she starts talking about donating money, and not just a little bit either. She wants to donate enough to establish—get this—a cancer center, can you believe it? We can't. Anyway, could you stop by and see her?"

Talk about a dichotomy, I thought as I entered her room. Was I about to encounter a generous, though eccentric, benefactor, or a needy, though cunning, welfare recipient? As it turned out, I met neither.

My initial impression of Sarah Stickler was one of a strong-willed, sharp-tempered, elderly woman, who knew her own mind and was neither shy nor reticent about speaking it. Physically, she was frail, but with terminal cancer raging through her ninety-one-year-old body, that was to be expected. There was definitely an eccentric side to her, however. Her gray hair was long and a bit unkempt. She was dressed in a stained T-shirt that she had pulled over her hospital gown. On her feet were torn, well-worn sneakers, and when she returned my smile, it was evident her dental hygiene would never qualify her for a toothpaste commercial.

As I extended my hand to introduce myself as the hospital's fundraiser, she began babbling quickly about finances, the national debt, and the world economy. When I posed a question in an attempt to follow her statements, she simply dismissed it, as she seemed unaware or perhaps she simply did not care about the courtesies of a routine conversation. For the next forty-five minutes, I merely listened.

Finally, in the distance, I could hear the dinner trays being distributed in the room next door. Knowing she would ignore my words, I took one of her hands and pressed it between my own. "Sarah, it's nearly time for dinner," I said. "I'll be back tomorrow to continue our talk. Is there anything I can get you before I go?"

She stared at me. Earlier, I had noticed she had no reading material, no television, and no telephone. "How about something to read?" I suggested. "A magazine, a book, a newspaper?"

In a small voice I heard her say, "Would it be possible to get me a copy of today's *Wall Street Journal*?"

In that instant, I knew she was genuine. Never once in my dozen years of gathering reading material for our patients had any one of them asked for a copy of the flagship of financial publications. Stained T-shirts, torn sneakers, and eccentric babbling aside, she was sincere. By the time I had returned to her room with the financial newspaper she had requested, Sarah was happily enjoying her dinner, while squirreling away packets of sugar, plastic utensils, and paper napkins into a shopping bag.

Arriving in her room the following morning with the current issue of *The Wall Street Journal*, I discovered another Sarah. Reading glasses perched on her nose, pencil clenched in her hand, she was busily adding columns of numbers. Suddenly, the eccentric patient had become the essence of efficiency and precision.

Looking over her glasses, she turned to me. "As of this morning, we have a little over $7 million. That should be adequate for our new center. I have already priced all the equipment we will need—two lineators (linear accelerators), a new chemotherapy unit, and a new holding areas for patients. It will cost nearly $7 million, and I want you to invest the balance. Also, I want you to name it *The Stickler Cancer Center*. Not that I want it named after me, but Stickler is a good name. When you are very sick, you want a 'stickler' to take care of you."

Then she paused and stared at me. "Do you know what 'stickler' means?" she posed. "Look it up. It will say 'one who insists on exactness and completeness.' Stickler is a good name for a cancer center."

It must have taken my brain several minutes to comprehend what she was saying. Swallowing hard, I managed to stumble to the chair beside her bed. Now it was my turn to stare. "Sarah, who are you?" I whispered, not knowing if I were addressing a visiting angel or an eccentric statistician. "How do you know all this?"

And her story began to unfold. "I know I am dying of pancreatic cancer," she began, as she held up her hand to quiet my protests, which she had correctly anticipated. "The same cancer that killed my mother over fifty years ago, is now killing me. It is disgraceful that in fifty years there have been no scientific breakthroughs, no discoveries to help people with this type of cancer. That is why you need to promise me that not one penny of my money will go to research."

Bitterly, she continued, "All my money is to be used to purchase equipment for this hospital. I have been a patient here for many years, and while your staff is excellent, you need new equipment, better machines to make the lives of people with cancer a bit easier. Right now, though, I need to check my research, I need to verify these prices. Do you have a buyer for cancer equipment? Someone in the purchasing department who specializes in this? Bring them here. I need to talk to them. But make sure they're smart. I don't have any time to waste with stupid people."

During the next forty-eight hours, I led a procession of purchasing agents, oncologists, radiologists, and hospital administrators into Sarah's room. In retrospect, I am certain they thought I was a bit loony, as I had overheard one of them remarking "our fundraiser seemed to have been taken in by a crazed woman," but I ignored their comments.

When Sarah was satisfied with the numbers both she and her parade of visitors had calculated, she seemed less agitated, more peaceful. That's when I asked her about her life, and her biography was a fascinating one.

She told me she was born on October 14, 1910 in Bayonne, New Jersey. Her parents, Samuel Stickler and Bertha Katz, were immigrants from Germany, who, in Sarah's words, "did not make a good marriage." The Sticklers had four children: Henrietta, Sarah, Teresa, and Charles. Listening to her, the marriage must have been a disaster, as Bertha, an Orthodox Jewish woman, took Sarah and her two sisters to another city to escape from her husband, whom Sarah had described as "a harsh man." None of the four Stickler children ever married, perhaps because they were too fearful of repeating the example set by their parents.

As a young woman, Sarah worked in the accounts receivable area of Bamberger's, the predecessor of Macy's department store, which was located in Newark, New Jersey. "We didn't make as much money as the girls who worked for businesses in the area," she recalled, "but we were able to compete for a weekly bonus."

Watching her eyes light up, I asked her about those bonuses. "Every girl was assigned a racehorse made out of cardboard," she told me, "and every day, your racehorse would advance depending upon how much business you could collect. By the end of the week, whosever horse was leading would receive the bonus."

I looked at her and smiled, "And I'll bet your horse won every week."

She gave me a high five and affirmed, "Every single week for three years!"

But winning a weekly cardboard horse race and accumulating a fortune of $7 million were still light years away. Sensing my interest, she continued her story. "I worked so hard at Bamberger's, and I saved nearly every nickel I made. But my family didn't seem to be getting anywhere. That's when I began to study how other people lived. The first person I noticed was the Irish milkman who lived in the apartment across the street. He worked hard, too, but he had more ease in his life. Then I discovered he owned the building in which he lived, and he collected rent each month in addition to his own pay. That gave me an idea."

By age eighteen, Sarah had purchased her first piece of real estate. A two-family house in which she and her family lived, the down payment secured by her weekly paychecks and bonuses provided by her cardboard racehorse. Two years later, she sold her two-family home to purchase an eight-family unit. Three years later, she traded up for a 16-unit building. By the time she was thirty-two years old, she owned over one hundred apartments.

But as her real estate holdings grew, so did her financial acumen. By the time she was twenty years old, she left the accounts receivable department and her cardboard racehorses behind, and headed for the broader world of financial markets. To her delight, she managed to land a job as an accounting clerk at a local brokerage firm. The ever-vigilant student, Sarah studied the traders and learned the mechanics of the stock market. Her instincts were uncanny, and she accumulated large sums of money. Then cancer claimed the lives of her mother and two sisters and she was devastated. Living alone, she continued to work hard, but became more and more reclusive through the years.

Listening to her story, I could not help but wonder if she had been a researcher in her youth, perhaps those suffering from pancreatic cancer would have had a higher survival rate by now. She had the ability, instinct, and drive to isolate a singular goal, focus upon it like a laser, and pursue it relentlessly, until she achieved it.

"That's why we need to establish this center, to give all of this some meaning. I suppose I could donate this money to a religious cause, but that's not what is important to me. And anyway, have you ever heard of a 'Jewish cancer'? I haven't." She paused to take a breath, then she looked at me. "Do you understand?"

I took her hand in mine. "Yes, Sarah, I do. We need to do it for all cancer patients, but especially for Bertha, Henrietta, and Teresa." Then I winked at her. "But we also need to call it something, and Stickler is a good name for a cancer center."

She smiled at me. "Yes, you understand. Please get me a lawyer."

Soon afterwards, Sarah signed her last will and testament, leaving nearly all of her worldly assets to the hospital. She established a small trust for her only surviving sibling, Charles, stating that upon his death, the proceeds would revert back to the hospital. Two days later, she lapsed into a coma and died. I was devastated. The young girl whose cardboard horse had won every race, the young woman who had amassed a real estate empire, and the older woman who had mastered every nuance of the world of finance was gone. I had known her less than five weeks, but in that short time I had grown to love her.

With the assistance of a local rabbi, I planned a simple funeral service the following day. At her graveside, the rabbi said, "Jewish tradition states the Messiah will come not in princely clothes, but rather in beggar's rags. Therefore, we are taught to look for saintliness where we least expect it. I know all of us who had the privilege of knowing Sarah Stickler have learned that lesson well."

Sarah's last will and testament was probated shortly afterwards, and at the time of her death, her estate was valued at $7.1 million. Barring the small trust, she left her entire fortune to the hospital. Everyone was astonished at the news—everyone, that is, but me.

Recently, the hospital broke ground to expand its oncology department, and people ask me if I had any idea what the woman responsible for all of this would have said about the project. I just look at them and say, "Stickler is a good name for a cancer center."

Somewhere I sense Sarah is riding a winged horse through the heavens.

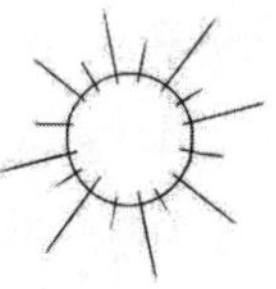

MOMENT BY MOMENT

When the mobile unit from the regional oncology center pulled into our quiet residential street last spring, all of us knew that our dear neighbor was coming home to die. Diagnosed with cancer months before, he had been a candidate for a radical, experimental therapy. Tragically, the treatments had not only failed, but accelerated the rate of the deadly growth. Having exhausted all other options, Don's last wish was to spend his remaining days at home. What we didn't realize at the time was that this very wish would teach our neighborhood how to live.

Several weeks before Don's homecoming, we learned our first lesson. Simply stated, the wish of a dying patient often means little if there is no caregiver, no partner, no spouse to make it happen. In that regard, Don was blessed with a loving, support-ive partner in Marian. During the months that both preceded and followed Don's homecoming, I often felt more sorrow for her as she shouldered, in many respects, a double burden. In addition to caring for the physical needs of her lifetime partner, she was coping with the emotional stress of facing her remaining days alone. Nevertheless, none of us ever saw her complain, cry, or break down during those last months.

Our next lesson was learned through observation as we watched Marian prepare their home for a terminally ill patient. One of the first things she did was move the kitchen furniture to another room. Initially the neighbors thought she had done that to accommodate medical equipment, but we were wrong. In that open space, she placed a comfortable armchair and ottoman near the window, creating a perfect view of the various bird-feeders, flowers, and late afternoon sunsets. Next, when she started to move the living room couch, we again assumed it was to make room for a hospital bed. But then we noticed she only moved the couch toward the center of the room so it would be close enough to the fireplace to luxuriate in the warmth. By this time, we knew enough to say nothing at all.

Then she concentrated her attention on bed linens, bath towels, and clothing. She scoured the department stores, mail-order catalogs and the Internet for the softest, plushest available. She finally settled on flannel sheets from England, Turkish towels from the Middle East, and a cotton blend of clothing from Scandinavia. Devoid of zippers, snaps, hooks, anything metal, this apparel was lovingly handmade with softness and comfort. Anything that resembled institutional linens or clothing would have no place in their home.

Next she directed her attention to nourishment. Shunning the medicinal protein shakes and liquid nutrients, she shopped throughout our local neighborhood stores for all of Don's long-time favorite foods. The weekend before his discharge, she had made rice pudding, chicken noodle soup, and beef tea. Her kitchen table was filled with bright bowls of oranges, nectarines, and grapefruits, and her freezer was stocked with boneless chicken breasts, baked ziti, and shepherd's pie.

The day before his homecoming, she dusted off their old record albums, and set up the hi-fi. To her delight, it still worked rather well, and seven long-playing records could be stacked up at a single time. Often throughout that summer, our local letter carrier told us he could hear tunes from the big band era wafting from the living room as he delivered mail to their front door.

The morning of Don's return home, Marian had risen early and walked to the local newsstand. There, she purchased our local paper, a weekly newsmagazine, and a crossword puzzle book. She added several new pencils, a felt pen, and a pad of ruled paper. She then stopped at our local florist and bought six red tulips, Don's favorite flower, and returned home to wait for her husband.

I wish I could report that Don arrived home and was miraculously cured, that a medical miracle had occurred, that home-made chicken soup had effected a cure that modern science could not, but I cannot. The disease that had been diagnosed as terminal did indeed take his life. But not immediately. Ironically, he was not even the first to die in our neighborhood that year. Tragically, another resident, a fifty-eight-year-old stockbroker, suffered a massive coronary and died one Sunday evening.

When the ambulance siren sounded and the vehicle raced up our street, all of us assumed it was summoned by Marian. But we were wrong. Don held on for another six months.

During that time, all of us were witness to a life that resonated with love, spiritually, and authenticity, a life that seemed incredibly simple, but had no time to be involved with petty insignificance. A life that celebrated each day, each hour, and each moment with joy. As all of us in the neighborhood visited with him that spring, summer, and fall, we developed a deeper appreciation for the simple pleasures and comforts in life—a hot cup of tea, a vase of flowers, a stimulating conversation, a sunset, a cozy fire, a red cardinal feeding in the snow. And those experiences had a profound effect on the entire neighborhood.

From my own window, I watched as additional birdfeeders began appearing in backyards throughout the area that spring. During the summer, I noticed more couples lingering outdoors hand-in-hand to watch the setting sun. As the weather turned cooler, I witnessed more smoke escaping from nearby chimneys, and in the evening twilight, I saw more of my neighbors hurrying home carrying bouquets of flowers along with their briefcases.

As the dawn of the millennium approached, I worried how Don and Marian would cope with the implications the new year would bring, but I need not have been concerned. I should have realized that God would be gentle with anyone who had treasured His gift of life as dearly as Don had. Early in the morning of December 30, which, ironically, was also his birthday, Don peacefully slipped away. I like to think God had called him home to celebrate.

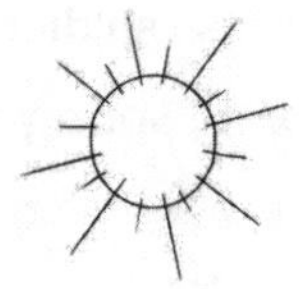

CHRISTMAS WREATHS IN MARCH

By the time the month of March rolls around, my body and spir-it are longing for spring. Somehow the cold, gray days of the cal-endar's third month are more trying on my soul than the equal-ly intemperate days of November. Perhaps my body is just tired of fending off the cold. Bleak January days and long February nights can be exhausting.

So when the calendar turns to March, I adorn my front door with a basket of spring flowers. Granted, these flowers are made of silk, but I organize a search mission for sightings of the real thing. And when I discover the year's first daffodils and crocus-es I cherish them, while celebrating each additional minute of daylight.

Of course, despite my optimistic attitude and best-laid plans, nature will conform to no one's timetable. Often, I sense her laughter, as it is not unusual to experience a snowstorm in April.

Yet, as I soldier through winter's final stance, I continue to incorporate spring into every late winter activity—until I notice a dried-up evergreen wreath on a front door, a rusty Santa on a March lawn, or blinking Christmas lights along bushes bordering the season's first forsythia buds.

In the past, I would characteristically explode, inwardly berating those people who choose to keep Christmas not in their hearts but rather on their front lawns. Was it laziness? Was it nonchalance? Was it uncaring? Why not welcome the spring? Why not let winter exit? What is wrong with these people? I could not understand such behavior.

That was, until I overheard a conversation in the local supermarket early one morning. Two elderly men were discussing the date—March 1. Both were widowers, one for several years, the other for only a few weeks.

The "new" widower was attempting to articulate his loneliness in the indirect manner men commonly do. "It's peculiar," he explained, "but I still have my Christmas wreath hanging on my front door. I just can't seem to take it down. My wife loved that wreath: the smell, the color of the ribbons, the pinecones . . . It represents the last Christmas we'll ever share together." He paused to wipe a tear.

"I know all about that," his friend responded. "My wife died in January, and I left our Christmas decorations up until April. Just couldn't bear to put them away, knowing she would never see them again."

Since that day in the supermarket, I have never looked at "delinquent" Christmas decorations in quite the same way. Now, whenever I seen a home bedraggled in holiday splendor in March, I recall that conversation. Perhaps the individuals in that residence are suffering from a similar tragedy. And if those decorations offer some kind of comfort or solace, some link to a happier past, well, so be it. I murmur a silent prayer, with the sincere intention that springtime will enter that home once more.

This story was originally published in *Whispers from Heaven for the Christmas Spirit*, December 2001.

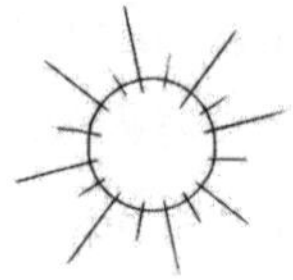

THE RETIREMENT

When Catherine Grzyrowski retired from her job as a laundry attendant at an urban hospital after forty-eight years of service, I photographed the event. To the casual observer, it was a pitiful, pathetic celebration. A cheap-looking sheet cake claimed center stage on a long, rickety table that had been set-up in a narrow aisle between rows of machinery. To make matters worse, because the heat generated from the nearby commercial washing machines and dryers was so stifling, the whipped cream roses that had adorned the cake were being transformed into puddles of pink icing.

That may have been a blessing, however, as I studied the scene more carefully. The greeting etched on the cake read: "Best Wishes on Your Retirement Katherine." A stickler for spelling, I cringed, thinking, why couldn't they even get her name right? Watching the roses continue to disappear into the script, I considered that maybe it was a good thing the wording would soon be rendered illegible. As my eyes traveled further down the "celebration" table, I noticed four Styrofoam cups stuffed with plastic forks, a roll of paper towels that would serve as napkins, and the faces of twelve sweaty coworkers who had stopped their duty on the laundry assembly line long enough to wish their soon-to-be former coworker best wishes on her retirement. I couldn't help but think poor Catherine deserved better.

While it was customary for the president of the hospital to deliver a few words to every retiree, on this particular afternoon the president was out of town. The respective vice presidents were also unavailable, so the highest-ranking manager would make an appropriate speech. Unfortunately, this particular individual was relatively new to the organization, and I had serious doubts that until a few moments ago he had even realized the hospital had its own laundry. His title was manager of organizational effectiveness, and most of us were still trying to define what precisely that meant.

Looking at him, I offered a silent prayer to laundry goddesses everywhere, but it seemed this prayer would go unanswered. As he approached the table, he seemed uncertain as to who the guest of honor was, despite the large corsage pinned to her uniform. He stumbled through a few trite lines on dedication, duty, and service, and thanked Catherine for her years with the hospital. His words were so bland, so inanimate, that they could have applied to anyone, but Catherine did not seem to notice. She was grateful and she smiled and thanked him, and proceeded to cut the sheet cake into neat squares.

In keeping with his earlier performance, the manager grabbed the first slice of cake, and began eating it as he hurried toward the flight of stairs that would take him back to his air-conditioned office. I doubted he would return to the department again.

Camera strapped around my neck, I continued snapping photographs of Catherine, her family, her friends, and coworkers. Though I had seen Catherine throughout the twelve years I had spent in the hospital, primarily in the employee cafeteria, I had never had the opportunity to really speak with her. That was about to change.

In halting English, Catherine was my tour guide as she escorted me down a personal memory lane, retracing her forty-eight years in the laundry. She showed me where she had begun her career—the start of the assembly line—sorting the soiled linens. Twenty years later, she was promoted to the soaping area, then the drying area, and, ten years ago, to the folding area. For the past five years, she was responsible for sorting the infant linens—basically receiving blankets, caps, wraps, and sheets. Listening to her, I doubted any high priest handled the vestments of a cathedral with more reverence.

With tears in her eyes, she told me how much she would miss her wonderful job. She told me about how much she would miss her coworkers, for they were like family to her, and how in the past forty-eight years she had never missed a single day of work . . . That remark startled me, and she explained she lived three blocks from the hospital, and, during the blizzards of 1960, 1977, and 1993, she had walked to work.

"You see, I had to get in here," she explained. "It was up to me to make sure the sick people upstairs and my babies have clean sheets, clean towels, and clean gowns." Though our tour was over, her words would stay with me forever. I thanked her, gave her a kiss, and promised to send her copies of the photographs.

A few weeks later, I was summoned to a special meeting held in the hospital's board room. Before the session began, I sensed this was no ordinary gathering. A buffet table was laden with crystal goblets of juice, croissants, fresh fruit, chocolates, and cheeses. Nearby, linen napkins, silver flatware, and English china plates were neatly arranged on a side bar. Somehow, this elegance was unsettling.

More disturbing, however, was the cadre of individuals attired in Brooks Brothers suits at the head of the table. With perfectly capped teeth, elegantly styled hair, and professionally manicured fingernails, they were arranging a laptop presentation for the management staff. In short, they represented a high-powered consulting firm which had been hired by the board of directors to work change throughout the institution. A new strategy was needed to improve the bottom line, bring in more business, and cut expenses. Simultaneously, this new direction would inspire employee loyalty, dedication, and service to the organization.

As public relations director, I was assigned to a special task force to identify "everyday heroes" throughout the organization to embrace this new effort. The leader of my task force was a rising star in the hospital, the new manager of the organizational effectiveness department. During our first meeting, we were to "brainstorm," and hopefully select a few candidates for this honor. Ironically, our leader had already put together his own list, which included the president of the hospital, the chairmen of the departments of medicine and surgery, the director of business development, who happened to be his own superior, and a handful of physicians.

It was then I spoke up, "What about a real everyday hero," I proposed, "just like the name implies. A hard-working, everyday employee, who comes to work, performs a job to the best of his or her ability, and is a source of pleasure and support to coworkers. What about an employee who even holds what could be viewed as a demeaning position? Someone who cleans soiled linens, for instance, and works in 100 degree heat, year after year, for say, forty-eight years, and has never missed a single day of work? What about someone like Catherine Grzyrowski?"

It was then the leader of our task force looked at me in disbelief. "That's not at all what this group is about," he responded with hostility. He then glared at me, muttered something about getting back on track, and mumbled under his breath, "I don't even know who you're talking about anyway."

It was at that moment I knew that not only our task force, but this entire project, was doomed to failure. If people like Catherine Grzyrowski were dismissed so unceremoniously, it did not bode well for the rest of us.

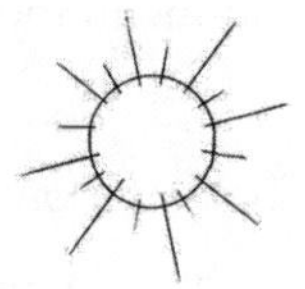

A Second Season of Miracles

When the director of engineering at the urban hospital where I work called me into his office several years ago, I was at a loss as to why. Having been employed for the past twelve years as the director of public relations, my responsibilities and his seldom overlapped. In the rare instances when they did, it was to open a new wing, pavilion, or parking garage, where public relations assistance was needed to communicate, commemorate, or recognize the feat. "We do the work, you arrange for the brass to take the bows," he used to joke with me.

Having knowledge of no new project in the works, I was curious as I walked into his sub-basement office as to what he had in mind. I didn't have long to wait.

Before I had a chance to say "Good morning," take a seat, or murmur any pleasantries, he asked, "Know 148 Palisade Avenue, the house between the hospital and the doctors' office building?"

"You mean the house everyone says is haunted?" I blurted out.

"That's the one," he smiled, rummaging through his desk. "We bought it—at least one half of it. It's a duplex and the family on the other side refused to sell. Holding out for a million dollars, I suspect. Well, they can just wait. When they finally get sick of waiting, they'll sell it to us, and then we'll level the whole thing. Expand the doctors' building. For now, it's yours. Use it for six months. By then, the owners will sell, and we'll raze the entire area. Put some kind of public relations program in there. Can't be directly related to patient care, though. The building is not zoned for it."

He paused, then added, "Oh, and you can only use the lower level. The first and second floors are not safe. When you decide what to do with it, let me know, and we'll paint it. Here are the keys. Good luck."

He tossed the keys to me, and I managed to catch them, but not my breath. "Put what in there!" I had wanted to scream. "A Halloween exhibit?" The house was an atrocity, an eyesore, a mess. What was I supposed to do with it? Host a black-tie gala?

But again, I was not destined to wonder too long. Sometimes the Universe has a synchronous way of working things through. Still bewildered, I headed for the hospital coffee shop, and ordered a large cup to go. While waiting, the hospital chaplain and the director of volunteers approached me. "May we run something by you?" they asked.

"Sure," I answered, sipping my coffee, "shoot."

Standing there, they explained that the neighborhood surrounding the hospital was in dire need of a thrift shop. An inexpensive, accessible place where residents could purchase clothing, household goods, and other items for little money. They even had a name for it, "Second Seasons." Volunteers would staff the shop, and the chaplain's office could solicit donations.

As I continued to sip my coffee, they went on to explain that the most pressing problem was finding a suitable location. It needed to be near the hospital, but no space could be allocated within the hospital building itself. Neighboring storefronts, while convenient, would be too expensive to rent. Did I have any suggestions?

Hearing that question, I cast my eyes upward, and half expected to see a celestial sign of some kind. Receiving none, I looked at the two of them, swallowed hard, and said, "Well, I know you're not going to be thrilled, and it's certainly not Rodeo Drive, but I do have a possible suggestion. How about we take a look at 148 Palisade Avenue. I have the key."

"The haunted house?" they said in unison.

"The very one," I answered. "Let's go."

Looking back, I think all of us were understandably horrified at what we discovered. The house had been neglected for decades, and the walls, floors, and ceiling were filthy, cracked, and peeling.

"We'll have maintenance paint, patch, and repair as best we can," I remember saying with more confidence than I felt. "The location is ideal—it's right next to the hospital. The neighbors can walk here easily, and so can the volunteers."

Listening to myself, I was amazed. Even to my own ears, I sounded like an aggressive real estate agent. Though I am certain they were less than pleased, both the chaplain and the volunteer services director agreed to "give it a go." I did not dare mention that the building was projected to be leveled in six months. Fifteen minutes later, I was back in our engineering department signing a maintenance order to have the basement area of the "haunted house" cleaned, painted, and repaired. Two weeks later, I was surveying the completed job.

While Nordstrom's and Bloomingdale's would never need to fear such competition, I was impressed with the transformation the hospital's maintenance department had managed to achieve. The walls and ceilings were patched, sanded and painted white. The floors were repaired and cleaned. An old cash register, no longer needed by the coffee shop, was set up on a countertop near the front entrance.

Later that day, the chaplain called me to report that a former patient was retiring. "And listen to this," he said proudly, "she happens to own a local department store. When I told her about Second Seasons, she offered to donate all the display cases and clothing fixtures—isn't that great? Maybe she'll even contribute some merchandise."

Free display counters, complimentary clothing racks and the possibility of a donation of new, unsold merchandise, certainly impressed me. Never in my entire working career had the pieces of a particular project seemed to fall together so effortlessly. I was waiting for the proverbial "other" shoe to drop, the one that spells trouble.

Again, I did not have long to wait. An hour later, the director of volunteers appeared outside my office. From her troubled expression, it was not hard to surmise all was not well. With words tumbling one after the other, she explained it was not easy recruiting individuals to work in the yet-to-be-opened thrift shop. None of the volunteers felt comfortable handling money, the cash register posed another challenge, and no one wanted to be responsible for reconciling the day's receipts to the cash taken in.

As for the merchandise, she continued, well, that was another dilemma. No one wanted to price it, no one felt comfortable displaying it, and no one knew how to organize the shop. Listening to her, my heart began to pound and my head started to spin. Once again, I sought refuge in the hospital coffee shop. While I sat sipping my cup of joe, one of the short-order cooks approached me. Shyly, he asked if he could discuss something with me.

Nodding, I smiled at him. He went on to tell me his wife, Josephine, had been recently diagnosed with multiple sclerosis. Because of her condition, she had to leave her full-time job as a cashier in a posh downtown restaurant. Now that she was home all day, she was becoming depressed, missing the daily contact she used to have with people.

Squaring his shoulders, he told me he had overheard several conversations concerning a possible thrift shop that might be established near the hospital. Then he asked me if I would agree to interview Josephine for a job as manager.

While it sounded like a perfect solution for my current predicament, the major stumbling block would be a salary. Under this scenario, I would need to pay Josephine at least minimum wage, and I was skeptical that the proceeds I was anticipating would cover it. Nevertheless, I agreed to interview her. What did I truly have to lose?

Intentionally, I scheduled our interview in the shop itself, as I wanted Josephine to experience at first hand what she would be getting herself into. While the area no longer seemed quite so ominous to me, Josephine had no idea how horrific the quarters were just two short weeks ago. Perhaps she would be dismayed by the stark walls and empty fixtures for she had been used to the ambiance of an upscale restaurant. However, I need not have been concerned, for as soon as she walked into the building, she was enthralled.

I hired her on the spot with the understanding that she needed to sell enough merchandise to cover expenses, including her salary. It was one of the best business decisions I ever made.

Under Josephine's practiced eye and meticulous planning, Second Seasons not only took off, it soared. In no time, she had the racks filled with clothing and organized by size, color, and season. The back area of the shop was transformed into a housewares and linens department, with everything neatly folded, stacked, or displayed. Then she created a children's department, where racks of the kids' clothing were cleverly interspersed with toys. This marketing technique enabled mothers to concentrate on their purchases, while their children entertained themselves nearby. Finally, she managed to effect a library corner, a jewelry department, and an accessory area, where pocketbooks, scarves, and seasonal items were displayed. On opening day, people were lined up outside the transformed "haunted house" patiently waiting to get in.

The first day, sales totaled nearly $175, which may seem meager to the casual entrepreneur. However, considering that a shirt sells for ten cents and slacks for a quarter, one can quickly develop an appreciative perspective. But even as the sales climbed, the most amazing thing to me was the volunteer staff Josephine managed to recruit. Like the former house that nobody wanted, these individuals could initially be described somewhat as "misfits."

For example, there was Daisy, who at ninety-two was nearly blind from macular degeneration; however, she somehow kept an eye on the cash register. Another volunteer, Rosa, who had suffered a debilitating stroke which left her partially paralyzed, would insist on moving the displays and bagging purchases for customers. And then there was Anna, who had severe bouts of depression after the death of her only sister, but could be found chatting with shoppers daily, advising them on their purchases. And overseeing the entire operation was Josephine, bustling and bursting with energy, kindness, and encouragement.

It was three years later, after Second Seasons was firmly established as a permanent fixture in the neighborhood, that a malevolent turbulence hit the healthcare industry. With increasing financial pressure, the hospital lost its family practice center, residency program, cardiac catheterization lab, and sub-acute care unit. As finances continued to slide, the hospital administration was forced to close a thirty-bed nursing unit, and seventy-five employees were laid off.

Ironically, throughout all of this chaos, Second Seasons (with a projected lifespan of only six months), continued to thrive. To date, the owners in the other half of the "haunted house" are still living there, and even if they wanted to sell now, the hospital no longer has the financial resources to buy them out.

As for Second Seasons, its doors continue to open every morning, sales continue to climb, and donations continue to pour in. And, even more miraculous, as goodwill, friendship, and kindness are nurtured within those basement walls, the negative effects of multiple sclerosis, blindness, paralysis, and depression continue to be held at bay.

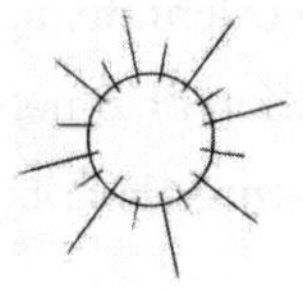

A Legacy in a Soup Pot

Have you ever noticed the busier your life becomes, the more empty it seems to be? . . . I remember staring at my date book early one Monday morning—scores of meetings, deadlines, projects leered back at me, assailing my senses and demanding my attention. I remember thinking for the umpteenth time, does all of this really matter?

And lately, with all this introspection, I've been remembering my beloved grandmother. Gram had a sixth grade education, an abundance of kitchen table wisdom, and a wonderful sense of humor. Everyone who met her thought it was so appropriate she had been born on April 1—the day of practical jokes, good laughs, and hearty humor—and she certainly spent her lifetime buoying up everyone's spirits.

Cerebral she was not, but to a child she was Disney World personified. Every activity with Gram became an event, an occasion to celebrate, a reason to laugh. Looking back, I realize it was a different time, a different sphere. Family, fun, and food, with nature also playing an important role.

Gram always loved birds. "If I could come back here as something else, it would be a bird—a big red one," she'd say. "Why?" I used to ask. "Because birds are beautiful. They fly like God's angels." So birds became a part of our routine. As a child I would accompany Gram, feeding pigeons in the park, songbirds in the garden, and seagulls at the shore.

Years later, I think I tried to recapture some of Gram's affinity with nature. One winter, to celebrate the solstice, I coaxed my husband to help me assemble an elaborate birdfeeder outside our kitchen window. For weeks, I'd fill it with "gourmet" bird seeds, only to have the squirrels scatter them. I had never seen a bird near the feeder, so I eventually stopped filling it.

But as much as Gram enjoyed her birds, meals were her mainstay—occasions to be planned, savored, and enjoyed. Hot, sit-down breakfasts were mandatory. The preparation of lunch began at 10:30 every morning, with homemade soup simmering, and dinner plans started at 3:30 p.m. with a telephone call to the local butcher to make a delivery. Gram spent a lifetime meeting the most basic needs of her family.

Stopping to pick up yet another take-out meal for dinner, my mind traveled back to her kitchen. The old oak kitchen table, with the single pedestal . . . the endless pots of soups, stews, and gravies perpetually simmering on the stove top... the homey tablecloths stained with love from a past meal. "My gosh," I thought with a start. "I'm over forty, and I have yet to make a pot of soup or stew from scratch!..."

Suddenly, the cardboard containers next to me looked almost obscene. I felt as if I had been blessed with a wonderful legacy and, for one reason or another, have never quite gotten to the point of passing it on.

The following day, I rummaged through the attic searching for a cardboard box that had been stowed away. Twenty-five years ago, that box had been given to me when Gram decided to move from the old homestead. I vaguely remember going through my "inheritance" as a teen. Every granddaughter had received a pocketbook, mine was a jeweled evening bag, circa 1920. I remembered I carried it at my college graduation. However, being a headstrong teen at the time of my "inheritance," I never really bothered with the rest of the contents. They remained sealed in that same box, buried somewhere in the attic.

It wasn't that difficult to locate the box, and it was even easier to open it. The tape was old, and gave way easily. Lifting the top, I saw Gram had wrapped some items in old linen napkins—a butter dish, a vase and, at the bottom, one of her old soup pots. The lid was taped to the pot itself. I peeled back the tape and removed the lid.

At the bottom of the pot was a letter, penned in Gram's own hand:

My darling Barbara,

  I know you will find this one day many years from now... While you are reading this please remember how much I loved you, for I'll be with the angels then, and I won't be able to tell you myself...

  You were always so headstrong, so quick, so much in a hurry to grow up. I often had wished that I could have kept you a baby forever... When you stop running, when its time for you to slow down, I want you to take out your Gram's old soup pot, and make your house a home. I have enclosed the recipe for your favorite soup, the one I used to make for you when you were my baby.

  Remember I love you, and love is forever . . .

Your Gram

I sat reading that note over and over that morning, sobbing that I had not appreciated her enough when I had her . . . "You were such a treasure," I moaned. "Why didn't I even bother to look inside this pot while you were still alive? . . ."

Needless to say, my briefcase remained locked, the answering machine continued to blink, and the disasters of the outside world were put on hold. I had a pot of soup to make, and for once, my priority was clear.

Hours later, after cutting, mincing, and dicing, a familiar odor began to waft through the kitchen. I closed my eyes. It was as if Gram were here again—I could almost feel her arms around me. I got up to close the kitchen window, as I didn't want any of this precious memory to escape.

At first, I thought I had imagined it, so I blinked. But it was still there, sitting in the middle of my empty birdfeeder, cocking its head, and staring at me . . . the most beautiful, brilliant cardinal I had ever seen . . .

This story was originally published in *A Second Chicken Soup for a Woman's Soul*, Health Communications, Inc., 1998.